Residual Sighted Children

By

Dr. Vimlesh Sharma
Department of Education
Shri Lal Bahadur Shastri
Rastriya Sanskrit Vidyapeetha
New Delhi–110 016

DISCOVERY PUBLISHING HOUSE
NEW DELHI-110002

Published by:

DISCOVERY PUBLISHING HOUSE PVT. LTD.
4383/4B, Ansari Road, Darya Ganj
New Delhi-110 002 (India)
Phone : +91-11-23279245; 23253475; 43596065
E-mail : discoverybooksindia@gmail.com
discoverypublishinghouse@gmail.com
namitwasan9@gmail.com
web : www.discoverypublishinggroup.com

First Published: 2003

Reprinted: 2022

ISBN: 978-81-7141-728-5

Residual Sighted Children

Printed at:
Infinity Imaging Systems
Delhi

PREFACE

Education opens up the heart and mind of young and old alike so that one can communicate and live in harmony and peace. It is the key to overall development of the society. Education is one investment which multiples the dividends manifolds as an unending process. It should be endeavour of one and all that the light of knowledge and education reaches one and all without exception—Prof. D.S. Kothari.

The education of handicapped children has to be organised not merely on humanitarian ground and to meet the demands but also on the ground of utility. Proper education generally enables a handicapped child to overcome largely his/her handicap and makes him/her a useful citizen. Social justice also demands it. It has to be remembered that constitutional directive on compulsory education also emphasises this.

Even, the Person with Disability (Equal Opportunities. Protection of Right and Full Participation), Act 1995 enjoins upon the government to ensure that every disabled child has access to free education in the appropriate environment till 18 years of age. It recommended integration of handicapped children with normal schools as equal partners, to prepare them for normal growth and enable them to face life with courage and confidence.

Of all the physical disabilities, visually impairment has been regarded as one of the most severe and traumatic sensory handicap i.e. partially sighted, low vision and children with residual sight is the part of this. There is a saying that of all the organs of our body, the eyes are the most important sense to gain knowledge, the normal child starts to learn most of the things by watching what is told to him or asking others. The blind child is, therefore, at a Considerable disadvantage in first three or four years of his/her life. The indicates the visual disability is a severe impairment in the personality development of the child. For example source of the knowledge are sense. If more than one sense are involved in the learning process, it will facilitate learner to comprehend the concept. In the blinds only audio sense functions in the learning process, whereas in the case of sighted persons, audio and video both sense functions. Therefore, they learn and comprehend more easily.

The present book is divided into five chapters and adopts a perspective approach to provide a comprehensive picture of needs of residual sighted children to integrated settings.

— The first chapter—Introduction—covers overview of the topic, Children with Residual Sight in India and its implications for education. National Policy on Education, Disabilities Act 1995, objectives, significance and description about the statistical techniques employed.

— The second chapter on Research Design includes plan and procedure of the study. Various steps involved in the construction and development of the test.

— The third chapter on Quantitative Analysis of Data comprises variables wise tabular presentation, application of statistics, analysis of data and discussion etc.

— The last chapter Findings, Conclusion, Implications highlights the results of the study, and would stimulate thinking on the part of researchers, teachers, special educators, parents of the children with residual sight, planners and policy makers to devise constructive programmes for children with residual sight in order to enhance their joyful learning.

The present book is a valuable document. It may also serve as a useful reference for classroom teachers, students working for the doctoral degree or administrator, who are interested in conducting research in special Education.

The information of this book will certainly encourage on the part of teacher, special educator and parents of handicapped Children to strengthen integrated education of residual sighted children and useful for those children who can not develop to their potential, without and additional help that can be provided.

I am grateful to many of the colleagues in the faculty of Education NCERT, NIEPA, Delhi University, Jamia Millia Islamia, JNU, and State Council of Education Research and Training etc. I am also undebted to various authors (Indian and foreign) whose book and articles I consulted during the preparation of the book.

I have no words to express my gratitude to my parents and dear brother Dr. Avanish Kumar, who gave me sorts of cooperation and inspiration and sustained me during the long periods of this work's preparation.

I feel privileged to express my heartiest thanks to the University Grants Commission, for the generous grant which proved to be a substantial assistance to me to complete the work.

Vimlesh Sharma

CONTENTS

1

INTRODUCTION

A sizeable section of population in any society is unfortunately afflicted with some kind of disability-mental or physical. The majority of so called 'normal population' do not hold, by and large, a very positive attitude towards the disabled individuals.

There has been a prolonged struggle throughout history for changing attitude of normal individuals towards disability. At one point of time in human history, it was considered a disgrace in certain societies to have a disabled child who could not be strong enough to become a warrior. Therefore, such societies had no place for disabled people. Such attitudes prevailed for many centuries till the time of the crusades, the great religious wars, during 1,000 - 1,200 A.D. Any disability became a symbol of punishment. It is a historical fact that 300 Roman soliders, when captured in a battle during the Roman Crusades, were blinded or partially sighted. Some people still think that disabled child was punished by God because he/she was sinful or the parents of disabled children were punished by God, because they might have committed some sin in then life. So the idea of sin, and misbehaviour and the idea that God retaliates and inflicts punishment, became associated with the public's attitude towards disability.

National Policy on Education and Education of the Disabled

Two recent developments have further influenced educational provision for the disabled in India. The Education Commission 1964-66 has underlined the neglect of their education in quantitative as well as qualitative terms. The Commission stated, "Not more than 1% of the mentally handicapped and 5% of the deaf and blind are receiving some education". Obviously the coverage is miserably low when compared to the coverage of even other weaker sections. It may be due to the fact that education of the disabled has been considered as a social welfare activity and not as educational enterprises. The commission, therefore, recommended a qualitative change in the conceptualisation of educational provisions for the disabled. Education of the disabled, according to the commission, should be developed as an integral part of the educational system (MHRD, 1985).

In the National Policy on Education 1986, education of the disabled has been emphasised in the context of providing equal educational opportunities for all. This section dealt with special groups of childern which need special efforts for educational development as they are educationally vulnerable. The objective of education of the disabled is to integrate the physically handicapped (including the visually disabled) with the general community as equal partners, to prepare them for normal growth and enable them to face life with courage and confidence (NPE 1986). The measures suggested to realise this cherished goal are—

1. Wherever feasible, the education of children with motor handicaps and other mild handicaps will be common with that of others.
2. Special schools with hostels will be provided, as far as possible, at district headquarters, for the severely handicapped children.
3. Adequate arrangements will be made to give vocational training to the disabled.
4. Teacher training programmes will be reoriented in particular for teachers of primary classes, to deal with children with special needs.
5. Voluntary efforts for the eduation of the disabled will be encouraged in every possible manner.

Regarding children with visual disability, one of the first things that educators have identified is the fact that children with residual sight are more like sighted children than unlike them. Research reveals that there are certain important developmental problems which occur on account of the child not being able to perceive the world in the same way as sighted Children do, but at the same time, after recognising that he is more like than unlike sighted children. We can identify the process of development of compensatory skills. If the child is taught the proper compensatory skill for learning, there is no guarantee that he will become self-sufficient, economically independent and emotionally adjusted adult but these are undoubtedly the means to reach the goal of independence. The concept of independence needs to be seen in a proper perspective. In other words, one of the primary goals of educator during the first three years is to teach the child how to study, how to acquire study skills, how to read, how to write, how to count and how to follow directions etc. Teacher should have faith in the capabilities of the child despite his/her loss of vision. Being a part of the community, he/she may need to modify his/her own reactions and attitudes. The parents of such children need counselling when required. Sensitisation of the peers and the community is required to correct stereotype behaviours and to build an encouraging climate for the child. The requirements are many and varying in view of the needs of the child; and the only asset to the teacher is his ingenuity, with which he may be able to overcome prejudices, unwarranted beliefs and behaviours to help the child with special needs to grow as a normal person as far as his/her potentialities permit.

Disability Act 1995

Some of the major recommendations of the recent Disability Act 1995 for the educational development of the disabled children are as follows:-

1. Research concerning the cause of occurrence of disabilities.
2. Promote various methods of preventing disabilities.
3. Screen all the children at least once in a year for the purpose of identifying all-risk cases.
4. Provide facilities for training to the staff at the primary health centres.
5. Sponsor awareness campaigns and disseminate information for general health, hygiene and sanitation.

6. Take measures for prenatal, perinatal and postnatal care of mother and child.
7. Create awareness amongst the masses through TV, radio and other mass media regarding the causes of disabilities.
8. Ensure that every child with a disability has access to free education in an appropriate environment till he/she attains the age of eighteen years.
9. Endeavour to promote the integration of students with disabilities in the normal schools.
10. Promote setting up of special schools on government and private sector for those in need of special education in such a manner that children with disabilities living in any part of the country have access to such schools.
11. Endeavour to equip the special schools for children with disabilities with vocational training facilities.
12. Conduct part time classes for children with disabilities who have completed education up to class fifth but could not continue their studies on a whole time basis.
13. Conduct special part time classes for providing functional literacy to children in the age group of 16 and above.
14. Impart nonformal education by utilizing the available manpower in rural areas after giving them appropriate orientation.
15. Impart education through open schools or open universities.
16. Conduct class and discussion through interactive electronic or other media.
17. Provide every child with disability, free of cost, special books and equipments needed for his/her education.
18. Provide transport facilities to the children with disabilities.
19. Removal architectual barriers from schools, college or other institutions imparting vocational and professional training.
20. Supply books, uniforms and other materials to children with disabilities attending school.

21. Grants of scholarship to students with disabilities.
22. Set up of appropriate forum for the placement of children with disabilities.
23. Make suitable modification in the examination systems.
24. Restructure curriculum for the benefit of children with disabilities.
25. Restructure curriculum for the benfits of children with hearing impairment to facilitate them to take only one language as part of their curriculum.
26. Ensure that all educational institutions provide essential facilities to blind students and students with low vision

Visual Impairment:

In the context of visual anomalies, children are often divided into two categories -

(1) ***the blind,*** whose absence of vision is so pronounced that they cannot be educated through visual methods and hence have to be educated through channels other than vision, and

(2) ***the partially sighted or children with residual sight*** who are able to utilise vision to some extent in acquiring educational skills.

It is important not to confuse low vision with partial sight. A Partially sighted child is one whose visual acuity is within the range 6/60 - 3/60 with or without a moderate field loss. A partially sighted child has special educational needs which are different from those of a blind child. He should be taught using sighted methods appropriate to partially sighted children. A blind child with low vision has a visual acuity of 3/60 or below, with or without a loss of visual field, or a visual acuity of above 3/60 with a severe loss of visual field. The blind child with low vision should be taught using a combination of sighted and non-sighted methods. He should be taught both to use sight and to manage without sight, depending on the circumstances. It is appropriate that totally blind children and blind children with low vision are taught together, as long as the different needs of the two groups are taken into account by the teacher. In the past it was thought that the use of low vision would lead to eye strain and to loss of sight. It was felt that sight should be preserved by not using it. This idea has now been abandoned and it is now felt that children with low vision should be encouraged to make the best possible use of that vision.

Children with useful low vision can be trained to use that vision better for mobility, daily living tasks and, possibly, reading. There are various exercises used to improve casual functioning. A training package entitled "Look and Think" helps children with low vision to develop methods for recognising common objects. It is often difficult to know how much a child with low vision can or cannot see. The use which they make of their vision will depend on factors such as age, experience, confidence, training. Clinical and functional assessments are important in helping the teacher to find out a child's vision. In addition, the teacher must observe the child carefully and keep a record of the child's ability to use his sight in different situations. The use of low vision will depend very much on each individual child. Children with low vision often need some training to make better use of their sight and to interpret what they are seeing. They can also be helped to see objects or features of the environment in three ways:

(1) Increasing the size of such objects or features;

(2) Lighting;

(3) Contrast.

Size

The size of an object can be increased in three says:

(a) The object can be brought closer to the eyes. This may result in tiredness and eye strain it done for a long period but it does not damage the eyes. If the object is held very close to the eyes, then the head can produce a shadow on the object, thus making it difficult to see the details of the object.

(b) The object can be magnified. There are many different types of magnifiers and it is important to choose the most suitable one for a particular task. Magnifiers also vary considerably in price and it is advisable to try out a magnifier before deciding to buy one. Magnifiers reduce the user's field of vision and it is necessary to slow down when using them. It is important to make sure that the lenses are kept clean and do not become scratched.

In addition to high-powered lenses mounted on ordinary spectacle frames, the most common types of magnifiers are:

Fig. 1.1 Hand-held

Fig. 1.2 Fixed on a stand without a built-in light

Fig. 1.3 Fixed on a stand with a built-in light

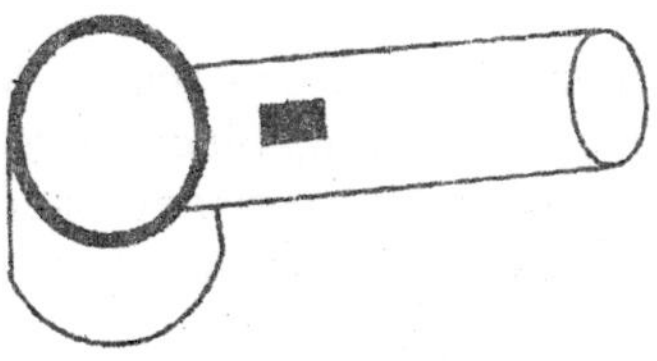

Fig. 1.4 Mounted on spectacles

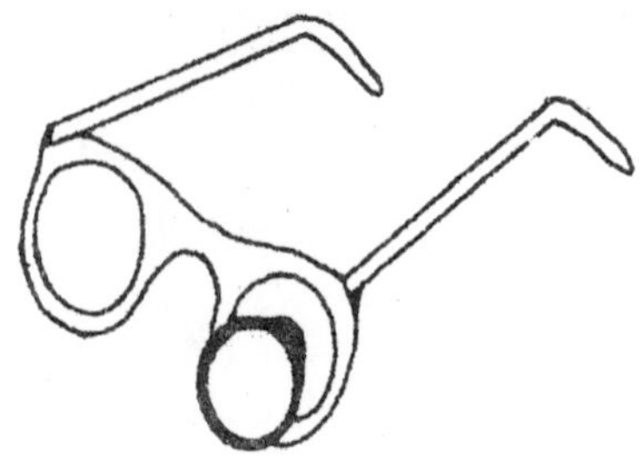

Fig. 1.5 Small telescope

Fig. 1.6 Closed circuit television (CCTV)

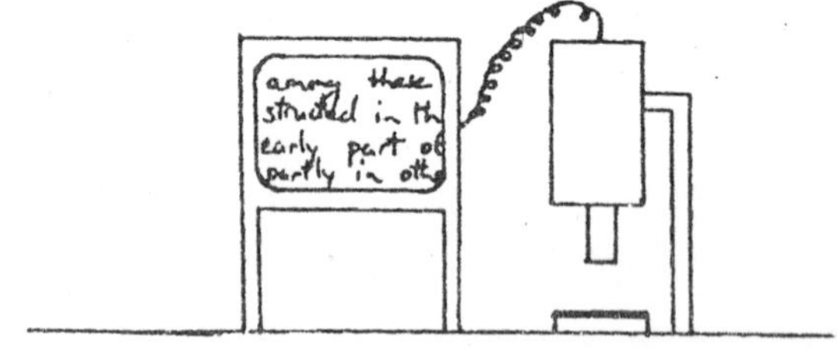

With the exception of the small telescopes, the above low vision aids (LVAs) are used mainly for reading. Since these low vision aids are expensive, it is important to compare the cost of an aid with its usefulness. In present-day the India hand-held magnifiers and those fixed on a stand are the most cost-effective. A child should have help in choosing a magnifier from a low vision aid specialist, who will also be able to give training in its use. In the absence of low vision aid specialists, teachers should take on the task of helping their children to experiment with low-cost low vision aids, especially for reading. Such aids can only be effectively used with adequate lighting. In many classrooms in Indian schools for blind children the lighting is not good enough for the use of low vision aids.

In mobility magnifiers are of limited use. A small telescope may be used for identifying such things as shop names and bus numbers. However, it is difficult to use and can only be used when standing still. It would be dangerous to walk around holding a telescope to one's eye. The telescope reduces considerably the field of vision and the user has to learn searching techniques, in order to find his objective. It is particularly difficult to use a telescope to find and hold on to a moving object, such as a bus.

(c) The object itself can be made bigger. This is not usually possible except for large print:

[illegible]
is over [illegible] indicating that the University
society. This demand is coming not only [illegible]
public service institutions, as the requests [illegible]
example. A further instance is the PTOC [illegible]
has been running since 1976, when it was [illegible]

Many books, mainly novels, are now available in English in large print. Books for young children also often have larger than normal print. It is also possible to make print larger by means of a special photocopying machine. In the classroom the teacher can simply use a felt tipped pen to produce large, clear handwritten material:

When using a felt tipped pen it is important to

It is also possible to buy large print items such as telephone dials and playing cards. Teachers of blind children should always produce pictures and diagrams in both tactile and large print form, in order to cater for the different needs of their children. Such material can be produced at low cost and should be saved for future use.

Lighting

If a child with low vision has to work in a dark room he will not be able to make use of that vision and will appear totally blind. Natural light can be very helpful to a child with low vision, as long as there is enough of it and it is not dazzling. In order to increase the amount of natural light entering a room, windows should be kept clean should not be covered with curtains. The walls and ceiling should be painted in a light colour to reflect both natural and electric light. Care should be taken to use paint which is not shiny.

In the design of new purpose-built schools for blind and partially sighted children, careful consideration should be given to appropriate lighting. While it is desirable that as much natural light as possible should enter a classroom without causing glare, this could well result in an increase in temperature in the room in the hotter months. In these circumstances, it may be better to draw curtains over the windows and to use electric light. However, in the winter months curtains should be drawn well back from the window. It is important to look at lighting in corridors and stairways, as well as in classrooms.

Ideally a room should have a mixture of general, background lighting and local lighting, where certain tasks are carried out. Fluorescent lighting provides a good spread of light throughout a room. For reading and other close work, local lighting in the form of a reading lamp is very effective.

Fig. 1.7

Make sure that the child does not trip over electrical wires when walking around the room. It is important to look at desk tops and other work tops: light, shiny surfaces produce glare, which can be very uncomfortable for a child with low vision and make it impossible to use that vision.

Filament bulbs must not be used without a shade, since they produce a lot of glare. Gas or kerosene lights are very bright and are not very suitable for children with low vision.

Fig. 1.8

Lamp shades reduce the glare from electric lights and help spread the light more evenly. They can also concentrate the light in a particular area. There are various types of lamp shades, which can be used for different purposes. Reading lamps concentrate light downwards and do not let light through the shades, which are often made of metal:

Fig. 1.9

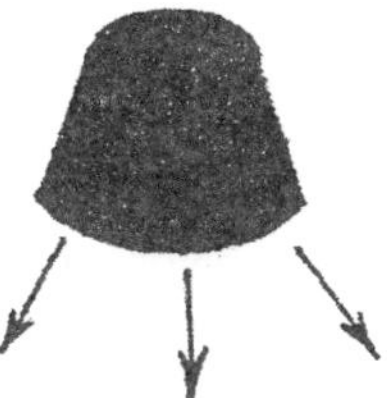

Lamps hanging from the ceiling should let light in all directions, including through the shade itself, which is often made of fabric or paper:

Fig. 1.10

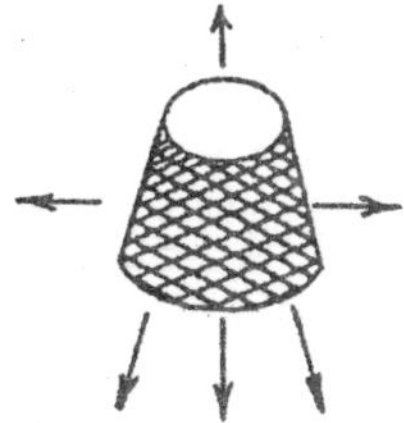

Contrast

Contrast can help children with low vision in carrying out many daily living skills tasks; however, it is particularly helpful in orientation and mobility. There are two types of contrast: colour and light /dark.

Contrast can either already be found in the environment or the environment can be adapted to make use of contrast. Which of the following doors in a corridor do you think would be most easily found by a person with low vision?

Fig. 1.11

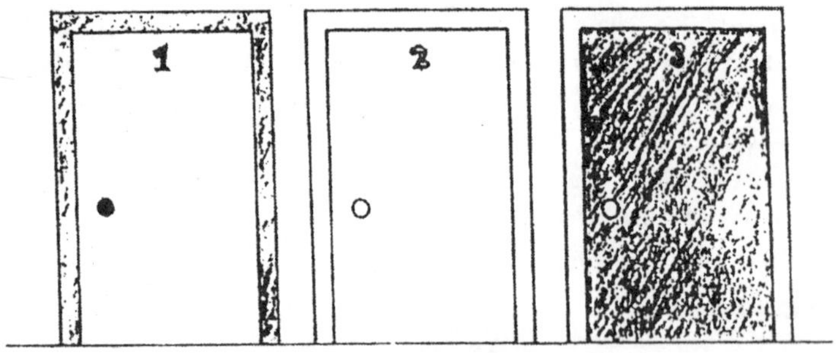

It is clear that door 2 would be very difficult to find, since it is the same colour as the wall. Both door 1and door 3 are much easier to find: door 3 is a different colour to the wall and door 1 is outlined in a frame of contrasting colour. Where doors and walls are of the same colour, the painting of frames in a contrasting colour can be a very effective aid to low vision. Similarly, when a dark coloured chair is placed against a light coloured wall it can be more easily seen.

Look around you and note down examples of where it might be possible to make simple changes in the environment to help the child with low vision.

Where contrast exists naturally, then the child should be taught to make use of it. For example, stairs going up can be recognised by the shadow which they produce.

Fig. 1.12

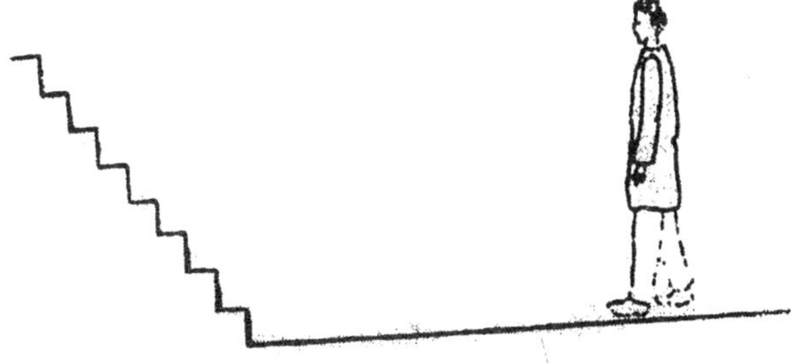

On the other hand, stairs going down are not easily recognised and can therefore be dangerous.

Fig. 1.13

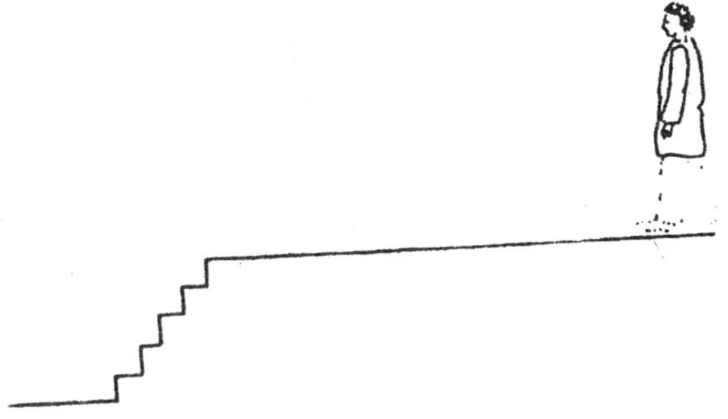

In order to help the child with low vision to find stairs down, a contrasting line should be painted on the top step. A similar line painted on the edge of each of the steps would provide additional help.

Outside the contrast between grass at the side of the road and the dusty road itself can act as a guide line, which the child with low vision can follow. The contrast may vary with the time of day: thus, a bright coloured wall may produce glare or may be difficult to see when the sun is shining on it:

However, when the sun is behind the wall, it will produce a shadow which makes the wall stand out from its surroundings.

A child with low vision may also learn to detect holes in the ground by the shadow which they make. As in the case of stairs-up and stairs-down, where there are pavements the kerb-up is much easier to find than the kerb-down:

Fig. 1.14

Fig. 1.15

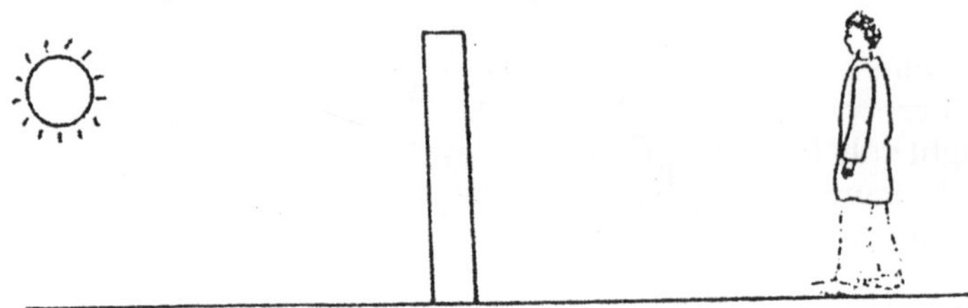

Fig. 1.16

Low Vision Training

While size, lighting and contrast are all able to help children with low vision to make better use of that vision, low vision training is also important. Children with low vision need help to interpret what they are seeing —their home, school, neighbourhood—all need to becomes places which they understand and are familiar with. It is part of the teacher's role to help the child with low vision to use that vision more effectively. This means that the teacher should work with children with low vision outside the classroom, in the area around the school, at the market and in the children's home area.

Low vision training is not easy because low vision varies so much from one child to another. Teachers need to observe their children closely, carry out functional assessments, draw up individual training programmes, experiment with size, lighting and contrast, and keep accurate records of their work. Teachers need to be particularly aware of the different needs of low vision children from totally blind children in the same classroom. It is important to ensure that the children with low vision are sitting in positions where they are able to make most use of the available light. The teacher should also take care that children with low vision do not become tired or uncomfortable as a result of using their low vision. Where this happens, children should be encouraged to use their sight only for short periods. In these circumstances, they will need to be taught to use both non-sighted and sighted methods and will need to learn to use Braille as well as print.

Blindness, Low Vision and Partial Sight

People without any vision or with very little vision are totally blind. Most blind people do have some vision, which may or may not be useful to them, depending on the task which they are doing. Some people may only be able to tell the difference between light and dark, while others may be able to see colours, shapes, outlines and even small objects. Lighting, contrast and the distance of the eyes from the object are all important. Some blind people may even be able to read print with the help of a special low vision aid; however, they will have great difficulty in reading and may only be able to do so for short periods. Although these people have useful low vision, they are still regarded as being blind.

People with low vision receive an incomplete or distorted image in their brain. Their ability to understand that image will depend on a number of factors unique to each person, including mental agility, experience and training. People with low vision see and understand things in different ways. Sometimes a person whose sight is slightly worse than that of another person may be able to move around and do things better than that person.

Partially sighted people have an important loss of vision: they are able to make use of their vision in carrying out a number of daily living skills tasks with the help of magnifying aids; however, their loss of vision will prevent them from undertaking those tasks for which good sight is required, such as driving a car. Frequently the special educational needs of partially sighted children are not understood because they appear to be "managing" by using their sight. Where such children are not given special consideration, they will often make slow progress in school.

It is important to remember that people with low vision and partially sighted people have a range of eye conditions and their ability to make use of their sight will vary greatly. Care should be taken not to make broad generalization about such people. They should be regarded as individuals with some sight difficulties in common.

Eye care

Ideally each school for blind children should have its own doctor and eye specialist employed on a consultancy basis. However, in India this may not yet be practicable. It is not enough to diagnose a particular eye disease; in many cases long-term eye care is essential. While the overall treatment of children's eye diseases is the responsibility of the eye specialist, the day-to-day care of their eyes should be undertaken by the school nurse. Apart from providing eye care, the school nurse has an important role to play in maintaining the general health and hygiene of school children, in giving first aid, in the teaching of daily living skills and in supporting both teaching and care staff. In the absence of school nurses, it becomes the responsibility of teachers to be aware of the need for eye care and to work closely with doctors in this area. Teachers should observe their pupils closely and refer any pupil with a suspected further loss of vision to an eye specialist. A loss of vision may be gradual or sudden, depending on the eye condition. The teacher should not attempt to make a diagnosis but should immediately contact an eye specialist. Prompt action may result in the saving of some sight whereas inaction may result in a total loss of sight.

The teacher should also be aware of the effects of different eye diseases on children's vision. Thus, albino children can become totally blind in bright sunlight and need dark glasses to protect their eyes from the glare. On the other hand, children with retinitis pigmentosa will become blind in the dark and will have difficulty in finding small objects and steps down. Those children whose retinae could become detached should not lift heavy loads or undertake vigorous physical exercise. Sometimes the insertion of drops n the eye can result in a temporary reduction in vision. Other types of medication also have noticeable effects on vision. It is important to make note of such effects and report them to the doctor. The ways in which different eye diseases affect children's vision need to be taken into account while planning the school programme.

Visual Acuity

Visual acuity is the ability to see detail. The visual acuity of people who are able to read letters or identify symbols is measured by means of a Snellen chart. The person whose eyes are to be tested sits at a distance of six metres from the chart —where a smaller chart is used this distance will be less (sometimes mirrors are used).

Fig. 1.17

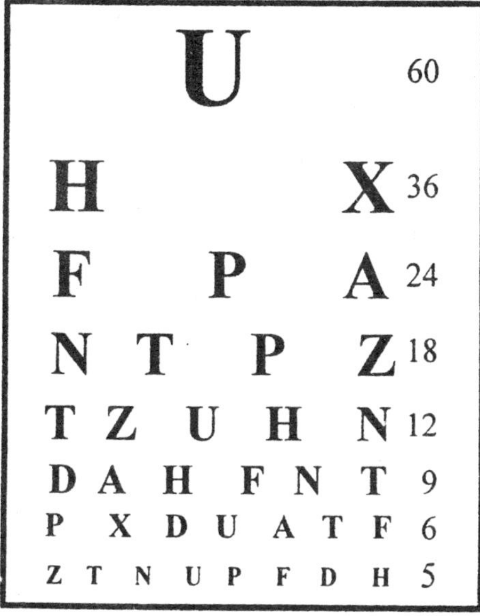

The aim is to compare the sight of the person being tested with normal sight. The eyes are tested separately, beginning with the right eye. Where a person wears glasses, his eyes are first tested without the glasses and then with them. The doctor, optician or health worker carrying out the test asks the person to read the letter or identity the symbol starting from the top of the chart. The examiner then records the number next to the last line which the person is able to see with ease. Where a person has such poor vision that he is unable to read the top line of the chart, he will be asked to move forward until he is able to do so. If the person is only able to read the top line at 6 metres, then his visual acuity will be recorded as 6/60 and read as "six over sixty".

The visual acuity in each eye is recorded separately and is often different: for example, R 6/60, L 3/60. It is important to understand that this is not a fraction: the figure on the left is the distance at which the person being examined is sitting from the chart (in the above example it is 6 metres when reading the chart with his right eye and 3 metres with his left eye); the figure on the right is the distance at which a person with normal sight would be able to see the same line - 60 metres. The person with 6/60 vision will be able to read the top line of the chart and is therefore not blind; however, he will have difficulty in seeing.

The World Health Organisation lists 5 categories of visual impairment: 2 categories of low vision and 3 categories of Blindness. For the purposes of this manual, people with a visual acuity of between 6/60 -3/60 will be regarded as partially sighted; those people with a visual acuity of 3/60 and below will be regarded as being blind. Although people with a visual acuity of 3/60 can see—they can see any object at 3 metres that a person with normal sight can see at 60 metres—their loss of sight is so great that they are regarded as being blind. The sight of blind people is categorised as follows:

- 3/60
- 2/60
- 1/60
- CF Counts fingers
- HM Can See hand movements
- PL Perception of Light:

  (1) with light projection—know the direction from which light is coming;

(2) without light projection—does not know the direction from which light is coming;

NPL No perception of light

Field of Vision

A person with normal sight is able to see the whole picture: when looking straight ahead he is able to see objects to the right and to the left, above and below. A loss in the field of vision means that part of the whole picture is missing. Different eye diseases produce different types of loss in the field of vision. The main types are Peripheral field loss, central field loss and irregular field loss. It is also possible to have a loss in one half of the field of vision. To determine accurately the extent of loss in the field of vision a special screen and special instruments are necessary, together with a trained examiner. In many cases loss of visual field is an on-going process, so that careful observation and regular testing are advisable.

In the case of a suspected peripheral field of vision loss, the following rough test can be carried out: the tester and the person being tested sit opposite each other; the person being tested covers one eye and looks straight ahead at the tester; the tester then holds one finger up to the side of the eye being tested; he moves his finger inwards until the person being tested says that he can see it; in this way, the tester is able to compare his visual field with that of the person being tested. This method cannot accurately determine the loss of field of vision but it can indicate the possibility of such a loss

A person with a peripheral field loss, commonly known as tunnel vision, will be able to see objects clearly directly in front of him (unless he also has a reduction in visual acuity). However, he will not be able to see objects to the side of him, above his head or below his waist, unless he moves his head. He will have difficulty in finding small objects or parts of larger objects and will have great difficulty in finding moving objects. He will have problems with mobility he will tend to stumble over objects on the ground and appear clumsy. He will have difficulty when moving from a light to a dark area. At night he will become totally blind. He will be able to read but will need constantly to move his head from side to side. He may find it easier to read smaller print rather than larger print. His field of vision will be limited further by the use of a magnifier.

Fig. 1.18

Peripheral field loss

Central field loss

Irregular field loss

Field loss in one half of visual field

A person with a central field loss should be able to walk around quite well, although he may be confused by the sudden disappearance and appearance of objects. He will have difficulty recognising people immediately in front of him. He will also have problems in reading and writing, since it is central vision which is used for these activities. He will also find it difficult to undertake tasks requiring hand-eye coordination, such as handicraft work.

A person with an irregular field loss will probably experience considerable difficulty in all areas of daily life.

Most people with a visual field loss can be taught to use their sight more effectively, while some people have taught themselves.

While young children may suffer from a visual field loss, it may not always be noticeable, since it may only cover a small area. Loss of visual field can continue very slowly over a number of years; sometimes it may come to a halt for a few years, while in other cases there may be a loss over a short period of time.

If a person has a large loss of his field of vision, he can be regarded as being blind, even though his visual acuity may be normal. In this case, he has lost so much of his field of vision that he functions as a blind person. However, in many cases a loss in the field of vision is also accompanied by a reduction in visual acuity.

Colour Vision

Colour vision is tested by asking the person to look at a series of coloured dots. It is not possible to use this method to test somebody with a substantial reduction in visual acuity. In the case of partially sighted people, it may be useful to know if they have difficulty in telling the difference between red and green. In the case on blind people with low vision, they will be able to recongnise some colours more easily than others: for example, yellow objects are much more easily seen than dark green ones—this has nothing to do with a defect in colour vision but with the nature of yellow as a colour. If you look at any distant scene, yellow objects will usually appear more noticeable than objects of other colours.

The residual sighted children are those children who have defective vision even after correction. Therefore, they need to be provided with visual materials and special methods of instructions. One important factor which distinguishes partial sight from blindness is the fact that while a partially visually handicapped child can utilise vision as an important channel of learning, the blind must rely on other approaches, primarily auditory and touch.

Identification of Children with Residual Sight

Generally, three methods are adopted to identify residual sighted children.

(1) Ophthalmological examination,

(2) Visual screening and

(3) Classroom observation.

The most authentic method for identifying residual sighted children is ophthalmological examination followed by medical check-up after brief and specified intervals throughout the school life of children. If ophthalmological examination is not possible, visual screening may be undertaken by the health officers, Sometimes classroom observation also proves useful for identifying the partially sighted children. One of the most important things that a low vision child should learn in school is to accept the responsibility of seeking help whenever needed rather than waiting for someone else to offer help. To assess the quality of work and to maintain discipline, the teacher best helps the low vision child by using the same standards that are used with order children.

Children With Residual Sight in India

India has a large population of people with visual disabilities. But various surveys conducted in this regard have yielded different estimates. The national sample survey of India in 1991 estimated the number of blind persons at about 4 million. But a study conducted two years earlier by Dr. Madan Mohan and World Health Organisation estimated the number of blind persons at 12 million which is the figure now officially quoted by the Ministry of Health. The same study estimated the number of persons with residual sight at 29.56 million. Thus in a population of 900 million, about 40 million people constituting about 3.5% of the population suffer from some degree of visual impairment. Table 1.1 shows major causes of visual impairment alongwith their secondary conditions and functional problems.

A multistate study conducted by a British team in 1994 estimated that India had about 200 thousand children of school age with severe impairment or blindness. The study indicated the following causes:

1. Staphyloma, scar and Phthisis balbi attributable to Vitamin 'A' deficiency in 18.6% of children.
2. Retinal dystrophies and albinism in 19.3% cases.
3. Micro-opthalmos, anophalmos and Coloboma in 20.7% case and
4. Cataract uncorrected aphakia and amblyopia in 12.2% children.

It is evident that different surveys have had a different focus. There are, therefore, different not in estimates to prevalence but also in the identification of causes.

Traditionally, blind and partially sighted children were educated together using Braille as the main medium of instruction for both. There was a widespread belief that using residual vision, could damage it, but experience and research in the past few decades have confirmed the view that its use improves rather than damages residual vision.

A development of far reaching importance is the distinction now made between visual acuity and visual efficiency. It is observed that in many cases persons with fairly low visual acuity and other limitations can function more effectively after they are provided training in visual efficiency.

The emergence of a wide range of visual aids and the techniques of producing print material in large print type have further improved the prospects of people with low vision. For the first time in India's history a comprehensive law on disability has been adopted by the Union Parliament. This act provides a statutory definition of low vision as follows:—

"A person with low vision is one who has impairment of visual function, given after treatment and/or standard refractive correction and has a visual acuity of less than 6/18 to light perception or a visual field of less than 10 degrees from the point of fixation, but who uses, or is potentially able to use, vision for the planning and or execution of a task."

The act promises access to education for all children with disabilities between 3 and 18 years of age. Currently India has very few low vision rehabilitation services.

TABLE : 1.1

CAUSES OF VISUAL IMPAIRMENT ALONGWITH SECONDARY CONDITIONS AND FUNCTIONAL PROBLEMS

Pathology	Secondary Conditions	Prognosis	Common Functional Problems
Albinism	Nystagmus	Non-Progressive	Glare/Photophiobia Nystagmus congenitally poor visual acuity.
Aniridia Cataracts	Glaucoma, on extent Nystagmus, Displaced Lens, Corneal Opacification	Dependent of under development	Poor light adaptation Glare / photophobia.
Aphakia	Glaucoma	Non-Progressive	Peripheral field distortion, loss of accommodation, poor depth perception.
Cataracts	Glaucoma	Progressive to total opacification	Scotomas Glare/photophobia constricted pupil.
Nystagmus	Usually is an accompanying condition	Non-Progressive	Possible fixation difficulty Reduced acuity.
Diabetic Retinopathy	Glaucoma Retina / detachment cataracts	Progressive	Gradual loss of vision fluctuating vision.
Glaucoma	-	Progressive and non-progressive	Constricted visual fields Night Blindness Light Adaptation.
Glare	-	-	Medication
Hemianopsia	-	Non-Progressive	Loss of half of visual field reading
Macluar Acgeneration	Cataracts	Progressive and non-progressive forms Stable	Loss of central vision scotomas
Optic Atrophy	Retinal detachments, Cataracts.	Progressive	Peripheral Field Distortions
Pathological	Macular Hemorrhaging		
Retinitis Pigmentosa	Cataracts Glaucoma	Progressive	Constricted Visual Fields Glare/Photophobia. Night Blindness.

We are beset with a number of problems in this area. India does not have the technology for producing aspheric lenses in acrylic which minimizes distortions. The aids available here are largely in glass and prone to severe distortions. However, an indigenous close circuit TV has been developed with a capacity for 30 times magnification. But the cost is prohibitive, at least for an average individual.

The education of children with residual sight requires considerable technological support, even with the best low vision aids, reading is likely to be slow, classrooms have to be specially adapted making it difficult for every ordinary school to provide the needed support services.

The following considerations are important in developing an education programme for children with residual sight.

1. **Training in Visual Efficiency**

   The visual performances of children with residual sight is not at the same level as that of sighted children. However, training in visual efficiency can improve performance.

2. **Reading Readiness**

- Minimising the effort in distinguishing the details of reading material.
- Management of lighting according to individual needs.
- Adjustment as size or type, spacing, quality of paper and use of illustrations combining print and pictures, self pacing of learning.

3. **Development of Listening Skills**

- Simple sound identification.
- Tonal and volume discrimination.
- Discriminating similarities and differences in sounds.
- Extending attention span and listening for factual details.

Despite training in visual efficiency, reading readiness and listening skill, our dependence on technology in educating children with residual sight is substantial. Fortunately, new devices particularly in the field of electronics are coming to our aid.

1. Interactive communication device.
2. Interactive classroom television system.
3. Variety of magnifiers like illumination, head-held devices, stand magnification, head borne devices, and electronic devices.

To being with residual sight children's education or rehabilitation programme may be located in urban centres, as even the better public school may not be in a position to provide the needed support services.

The Education Commission (1966) had recommended establishment of special schools for more severely-disabled children. Although children with residual sight cannot be regarded as severely disabled, the support services needed warrant their education in a special environment. Some research suggests that the prevalence of learning difficulties among low vision children is much higher than in a cross section of a population of sighted children. Thus, it may be necessary not only to deal with the special problems as low vision, but also with some basic problems of dyslexia, dysgraphia and other learning difficulties. A number of strategies for coping with these problems are being developed. It will be necessary to use a combination of strategies alongwith a multi sensory approach to cope with educational problems of low vision children.

Concept of Cognitive Style

Cognitive style, a psychological construct, characterizes individual differences in styles of perceiving, remembering, thinking and judging. The term cognitive style refers to the characteristic way in which individuals conceptually organise the environment. Cognitive style was viewed by Kogan, Moss and Sigel (1963) as "stable individual preference in mode of perceptual organization and conceptual categorization of the external environment.

Cognitive style as defined by Witkin (1971) is the characteristic self-consistent mode of functioning which individuals show in their perceptual and intellectual activities. These cognitive styles are manifestations in the cognitive sphere of still broader dimension of personal functioning which cuts across diverse psychological areas.

There are different kinds of cognitive styles like sharpheres and levelers, narrows and extensive scanner, psychological differentiation, tolerance/intolerances for ambiguity, field dependence and Independence for ambiguity, cognitive Consistency and locus and control (Forgues and Shulman 1979). The field dependent and independent conceptualisation to Witkin and his colleagues has generated, by far, the greatest amount of research. This research and theorizing has extended the original perceptual style concept into cognitive and social domains.

The extended conceptualisation implicates field dependence and independence as aspects of more generalised individual difference dimension which is defined as one extreme by globle. (non-analytic) approach to the field and at the order extreme by a highly articulated analytic approach to the perceptual or conceptual field.

Witkin noted the individual's characteristic way of perceiving was consistent from one situation to another, that it was not easily altered, and that is in a way stable over a period of time. It has been demonstrated that people who are field dependent in the area perceptual situation tend to be field independent in their perceptual and problem solving situation as well. Individuals differ very much in all aspects of their personality and thus various methods and techniques have been developed by researchers, educationists and psychologists, to indentify individual differences. Identifying student's cognitive style is one such method which may be used for individual instruction.

Cognitive style may be referred specially to a person's characteristic pattern of behaviour in a particular learning field. The determination of functional levels and specific deficits provides the essential information in deciding 'what' a child should be taught and deciding 'how' to teach him effectively requires a different data base.

A number of psychologists, educationists and researchers have defined the term 'Cognitive style' as a potential individual difference that may be used by the teacher to enhance student's learning. The term cognitive style refers to a way or approach, a student follows on his course of learning, Rebeck (1973) has defined it as the individual's tendency to function intellectually in a way he has succeeded. Laycock (1978) describes cognitive style as an individual's characteristic way of responding to certain variables in the instructional environment. However, to state it more briefly a student's cognitive style is the way with which he learns best. Sigel and Coop (1974) have viewed Cognitive style as an integral concept that bridges cognitive dimension of individuals personality. Gibson (1976), on the other hand, argues that cognitive style and learning style as synonymous and defines cognitive style as the different ways in which people process information in the course of learning. Asubel (1966) , Dececco (1974), Messick (1969) and Kogan, Moss and Seigal (1963) also felt that learning style and cognitive style are synonymous which include individual preference in both perceptual organisation and concept categorisation that is perceiving, thinking, remembering and solving problem.

So cognitive style represents patterns of individual variation in the mode of perceiving, remembering and thinking which is to be reflected with consistency in a wide range of learning and social situations.

Definitions of Cognitive Style

Kogan, Moss and Sigel (1963 p. 74) referred to cognitive style as under:-

"Among children of adequate intelligence there are those who characteristically analyse and differentiate the stimulus field, applying labels to sub-elements of the whole, others tend to categorise a relatively undifferentiated stimulus. Some children are splitters, other are lumpers."

Messick (1976) defined cognitive styles in terms of consistent patterns of "organizing and processing information. Zojnoc (1968) similarly maintained that cognitive structures mediate between environmental input and the organism's output. He added that Cognitive structures organise behaviour as well as input.

Coop and Sigel (1971) used the term cognitive style "to denote consistencies on individual modes of functioning on a variety of behaviour situations". This definition is, as Coop and Sigel pointed out, similar to the use of the term 'style' by Gordon Allport (1937) to describe consistencies of behaviour.

Goldsteim and Blackman (1978) define cognitive style as a hypothetical construct that has been developed to explain the process of mediation between stimulus and response. Here the term cognitive style refers to the characteristic ways in which individuals conceptually organise the environment.

The above discussion shows that cognitive style has been viewed from different angles.

TABLE : 1.2

VIEWS OF COGNITIVE STYLE

Style type	Integrated A+B	Style A	Style B	Under-developed	Author
Perceiving	-	Field-dependent	Field-independent	-	Witkin
	Fast, accurate	Impulsive	Reflective	Slow, inaccurate	Kagan
Information	-	Broad	Narrow	-	Wallach
Processing	-	Rational	Analytic	Descriptive	Kagan
Concept Thinking	Both strong	Divergeers (imaginative)	Convergers (Logical)	Both weak	Hudson
Learning	Versatile	Holistic	Serialist	Rote	Pask
Personality	Integrated	Expressive Emotional Cognitively Complex	Self-Contained Inhibited, Practical	-	Hudson Entwistle and Morison

Source – International Encyclopeadiea of Education adopted from Entwistle (1981) p.218.

Witkin et. al (1971) pp.14-16 has summarized in general some essential characteristics of cognitive style. They are as follows.

1. Cognitive styles are concerned with the form rather than the content of cognitive activity. They refer to individual difference in how we perceive, think, solve problems, learn, relate to other, etc.

2. Cognitive styles are pervasive dimensions. They cut across the boundaries traditionally used in compartmentalizing the human psyche and so help restore the psyche to its proper status as a holistic entity. Reflecting their pervasiveness, cognitive style carries a message about

what we traditionally call 'personalitites'. So it is a feature of personality and not only of cognition in the narrow sense.

3. Cognitive styles are stable over time. This does not imply that they are unchangeable. Indeed, some may easily be altered. In the normal course of events, however, we can predict with some accuracy that a person has a particular style one day, month, and perhaps even years later. This stability makes cognitive style useful particularly in long range guidance and counselling.
4. With regard to value judgement, cognitive styles are bipolar. This bipolarity makes it less threatening and therefore easier to communicate information about an individual's cognitive style directly to him than it is to convey some information about his abilities, as for example, telling him he has a low IQ.

A brief description of different cognitive styles identified by psychologists and researchrs is presented below:—

1. Flexibility Vs Non-Flexibility

The students who are not satisfied with traditionally accepted solution to a learning problem and always try to arrive at unique responses and solutions are said to be having flexible cognitive style. On the other hand, students who are satisfied with traditionally accepted response to a learning situation are stated to be having non-flexible cognitive style.

2. Individualistic Vs Non-Individualistic

Students who are self-centred or independent on their learning possess individualistic cognitive style. On the other hand, students who require help or assistance possess non-individualistic cognitive style.

3. Modality Preference—Aural Vs Visual

This refers to an ability to learn and retain information more effectively when certain channels of communication are employed. Students differ with respect to how much they rely on 'eyes' or 'ears' for learning. Some students prefer those subjects in which some type of visual aids are used and they have to perform or construct something. These students are said to be having aural cognitive style. On the other hand, students having aural cognitive style prefer those teachers and subjects which require them only to listen. They remember best only when they themselves speak it or hear it from someone.

4. Field Independent Vs Field Dependent

Learning is influenced by the structurisation of learning situation. This type of learning is called field dependent but there are students who grow in their learning at their own and do not care for the structurisation of learning task provided to them. This type of learning is called field-independent.

5. Short Attention Span Vs Long Attention Span

Attention span does influence learning of students as they vary in their capacity to concentrate for a short or long duration of time in their learning tasks. When a task is given some students work on till it is completed. They can continue or sit long without getting bored or without taking some type of intake in between. Such students are stated to be having long attention span cognitive style. On the other hand, some other students are stated to be having short attention span cognitive style as they experience difficulty in concentrating for a long time during their learning. They lose interest, get irritated and get involved in social activities rather than completing their learning task.

6. Motivation Centred Vs Motivation Non-centred

Motivation centred students are eager to learn, they should be told exactly what they are required to do, what resources are available to them, how to get help if they need, if and how they will be expected to demonstrate that they have learnt what they were assigned. Students who are motivation non-centred rarely succeed in life. They do not work hard and blame others for their failures and always feel disappointed.

7. Environment Oriented Vs Environment Free

There are some individuals who are quite sensitive to physical environment features, i.e. sound levels, conversations, street noise and other distractions and prefer to learn in a quite cogenial environment. They have been termed as having environment oriented cognitive styles. On the other hand, there are students who do not bother for such type of disturbance and can concentrate on their learning task undisturbed. For example, music does not affect their concentration.

8. Responsiblility Vs Irresponsibility

Responsible students are those who obey their teachers, do their work in time, help school authorities in maintaining discipline and the like. Irresponsible students, on the other hand, try to create disturbance in classroom, neither do work themselves in the classroom nor let others do their work and try to create problems for school administration.

Concept of Achievement

In a layman's perception, academic achievement refers to student performance in various curriculur subjects in educational institutions.

Achievement means accomplishment or proficiency of performance in a given skill or body of knowledge. Random House Dictionary of English language defines academic achievement as something accomplished especially by superior ability, special effort and great valour, "A test of educational achievement is one designed to measure knowledge, understanding, skills in a specified subject or group of subjects".

Academic achievement is an index of the amount learned during the course and results of final examination to be the best indicator of amount learned, even though individuals were not equal in proficiency at the beginning of the learning task. Based upon several considerations, it was concluded that, at present, the best indicator of amount learned in many classroom situations is the grades or results of the final examination. Thus it is clear that any teacher or employer can very easily ascertain the knowledge of the subject matter and amount of knowledge learned by a student during his/her course. Higher grade in the class will be an indicator of high achievement. It is also evident from this finding that better grades will facilitate promotion to the higher class and also getting employment.

By its very nature education is experimental. There are some perennial questions which keep the teacher and curriculum planner baffled: 'what is the key to academic succes' is one of the baffling questions that has engaged the attention of education researchers. Success in school or college is a good indication of probable success in later life.

Achievement is one of the most important criteria on the basis of which students are channelised to different streams of life. In modern competitive society, academic achievement occupies an important position in human life. The keen competition among the participants and entrants in any profession has made the need for good academic career still more important. A low academic achiever has a very poor chance of suitable employment. The admission in higher institutions is primarily given on the basis of the percentage of marks obtained in earlier courses of study.

The value of academic achievement is reflected in its role for admission to higher education courses on the one hand and employment on the other. Consequently pressure on school and college going students for high academic achievement has increased tremendously. Parents have become more conscious about higher academic scores in examination as they have realised that their wards would be left without a suitable job even after spending a number of years in school and college and consuming the meagre economic resources of an average Indian family. Therefore, parents arbitrarily fix some unrealistic standard of academic achievement for their children consciously or unconsciously without due consideration to their capabilities.

The Problem - Need and Justification

The Education Commission (1964-66) states that the education of handicapped children has to be organised not merely on humanitarian ground and to meet the demands but also on the ground of utility. Proper education generally enables a handicapped child to overcome largely his/her handicap and makes him a useful citizen. Social justice also demands it. It has to be remembered that the constitutional directive on compulsory education also emphasises this. The National Policy on Education (1986) states that there is a need to integrate the handicapped children with general community as equal partners, to prepare them for normal growth and enable them to face life with courage and confidence but life is very competitive and sensory, motor, emotional or intellectual impairment of the handicapped persons is something which holds them back in competition with other people.

Of all the disabilities, blindness has been regarded as one of the most severe and most traumatic sensory handicaps. There is a saying in Sanskrit 'Sarven Dhrivanam Nayanam Pradhanam' which means of all the organs of our body the eyes are the most important sense to gain knowledge. The normal child starts to learn most of the things by watching what others do, but the blind child has to learn by listening to what is told to him or by asking others. The blind child is, therefore, at a considerable disadvantage in first three or four years of his/her life. This indicates that visual disability is a severe impairment in the personality development of the blind child.

Cognitive styles, by embracing both perceptual and intellectual domain and by their frequent implications in personality and social functioning promise to provide a more effective characterization of student's mental function than it could be provided by intellectual tests alone. This characterization should have relevance not only for the course of individual learning in various subject matter areas, but also for the nature of teacher-pupil interaction and the social behaviour in the classroom.

Thus, cognitive styles by virtue of their widespread operations appear to be particularly important dimensions to assess for educational purposes, yet, the very pervasiveness that under-scores their importance at the same time interferes with the measurement of other important personal characteristics such as dimensions of specific aptitudes and interests. This is because cognitive styles operate in testing situation as well, and frequently interacts with test format and test conditions and influence the examinees' score.

In the areas of teaching learning, knowledge about cognitive style offers a number of opportunities of its use, but choices among them depend upon particular education goals (and upon the much needed empirical research). For example, as soon as we are able to assess the cognitive styles of students, we have the option of placing them in classroom in specific ways, perhaps in homogeneous grouping, which is uniformly beneficial. In the recent study of ability grouping in New York city school, high ability students over the course of a year were found to gain an average of 20.7 months of the norms of word knowledge test when in homogeneous groups but an average of 14.7 months in heterogeneous classes, perhaps the teaching procedure is geared to the homogeneous low ability students who learn from their brighter peers in heterogeneous classes or view their excellence as a standard for personal striving.

It is desirable to assess cognitive styles of teachers to consider the possibility of assigning them to students to obtain particular combinations of styles that would optimally fasten the pace of learning. We could also consider selecting a particular teaching method that would be specially appropriate for certain cognitive styles and certain subjects.

There is need to study cognitive styles of children with and without residual sight in relation to their achievement in different areas. However, the result obtained for boys may not be applicable to girls. Therefore, difference in the achievement of boys and girls with normal sight are residual sight needs to be studied separate.

The findings of the study would provide a frame of reference for curricular development and would supply relevant data regarding cognitive processes that would not only help in integration and assimilation of information but would also help in evolving a hierachy of contents of the subject and could be of great help in improving these conditions for better development of their personalities.

The accumulated knowledge of the past provides the base on which the edifice of new knowledge is to be created. Hence, the present section purports to go deep into the accumulated knowledge of the past in the field of cognitive styles and achievement. The purpose of reviewing the earlier researches is not only to economise the historical perspective of the present work but also that the related studies that have taken cognizance of one or more variables included in this study and as such these studies may help the investigator to design here study in a manner such that recurrence of the shortcomings and pitfalls observed in any earlier study may be checked. Alternatively, their findings may be utilized to substantiate and support, wherever necessary, the interpretation of the results of the present study.

The investigator made a survey of the literature related to the present work and came to the conclusion that not many researches of this type have been carried out in India. However quite a few studies of the type have been carried out abroad. The studies related to one or the other specific objective laid down in the present study are also available. No single study could be located which encompasses all the aspects of the present work. Hence, the studies available in this field are partially related to the present problem. Therefore, for convenience only those studies have been reviewed by the investigator which have a relevance with one or the other variables of this study. The studies are reviewed under two categories.

- **Studies on Cognitive style.**
- **Studies on Achievement.**

Data on the cognitive style and education achievement of children with residual sight are extremely limited. In contrast to the dearth of educational and psychological research on children with residual sight, there are extensive medical reports, numerous studies on relations between very minor visual defects and reading disabilities, and many reports of personal experiences and opinions based on work with partially sighted children. The following need to be noted with regard to children with residual sight:

1. The child with residual sight is truly the neglected child in special education.
2. The estimated rate of 1/500 is too high to be meaningful.
3. The partially sighted children generally do not experience an eductional problem of such magnitude that special education becomes necesary for them. The early studies of Myers (1930) and Pintner (1942) both found more partially seeing children with achievement below 90 and fewer with above 109 than would be expected on the normal distribution. Myers reported achievement test scores for 709 partially seeing children and found almost 60 per cent to be below 90 and only 9 per cent above 109. Pintner repored 41 per cent below 90 and 17 per cent above 109 in a study of achievement of 602 partially sighted children from 10 to 12 years of age. The mean for achievement for Pintner's group was 95,1 and the median was 93.

Livingston (1958) confirmed Printer's finding that enlarging the test materials did not increse the scores obtained by partially sighted children when he compared the performances of 60 partially seeing children with those of normal children. Mueller (1962) found that enlarging the Peabody picture vocabulary test pictures did not significantly increase the scores of partially seeing children.

The only study available which comes even close to comparing and contrasting educational achievement and intelligence for the partially sighted children and normal seeing children is an exploratory one by Bateman (1964). No differences were found in school achievement in relation to other partially seeing children.One third of the children were rated below average, 44 per cent average, and 23 per cent above average. However, when teachers were asked to rate partially seeing children in relation to normal children, their ratings changed to 45% below average and only 15 per cent above average. The implication of this appears to be that teachers of partially seeing children perceive them as achieving less well than do normal children, even Peck (1933) found reading of partially seeing children to be at grade level, but two more recent studies (Eakin, Pratt, McFarland 1961, Nolan 1959) found slower than average reading among this group. Bateman (1963b) found that the partially seeing children studying in grade 3 and 4 read less than 1/2 month below grade placement according to normal norms on the Gates silent reading comprehension tests. They read an average of 6 months below Binet Mental age. However, as a group, their speed of reading was only about 2 months below their own comprehension and word-recognition level. The types of reading errors made did not differ substantially from those made by normal children of comparable reading levels. Accuracy of reading among the partially seeing was higher than it is for normally seeing. The slight reading retardation found in the partially seeing group was attributed to a small group of children with very mild visual defect, most of which was refractive problem.

Eakin, Pratt and McFarland (1961) analyzed the studies of type size and style used by children with residual sight and concluded that

1. 24-point type is preferable to 30-point type.
2. More partially sighted children can read 24-point type than children who can read smaller type.
3. There is only inferential support for maintaining that 24-point type is read as fast as 18-point type.
4. Partially seeing children read faster than the legally blind. In general, each child should read the smallest type he can handle without discomfort in order to maximize his

potential speed of reading and the availability of materials to be read. Since the provision of books printed in large type constitutes one of the major educational modifications for this group of exceptional children, every effort should be made to have the necessary materials available on appropriate type size.

Review highlights– The following conclusions can be drawn from the review of literature.

1. Learning is a phenomenon that goes in and outside the four walls of the school, formal learning is considered important in school. In school, the total environment inclusive of organizing various curricular and co-curricular activities plays an important role in shaping student behaviour with regard to cognitive and non-cognitive factors.
2. Cognitive style is bipolar on the one hand. There are fexible, field independent, individualistic, motivation oriented and short and long attention span people who are more analytic and hence prefer subjects and vocations which are of impersonal nature and which require analytic and problem solving skills. At the other end of the continuum are non-flexible, field-dependent, non individualistic and motivation free people who are less analytic or global and hence prefer subjects requiring interpersonal qualities and less analystic abilities.
3. Children with special needs perform better in mathematics and languages with the present ways of teaching these disciplines.
4. Cognitive style is related to the development level of the person. Between the age of 10 and 12 years, 1Q sharply increases, while it increases slighly between the age of 14 to 18 years, after that no significant effect of change of age is visible, for older people it decreases again (in both the sexes) because of their inaccuracy on perception (Eisner 1972).
5. Few researches seem to be carried out on relationship of the cognitive style with achievement with reference to children with special needs.

In the light of conceptual framework discussed the investigator decided to undertake a study which has been titled as -

"Cognitive Styles of Children with and Without Residual Sight and Their Achievement in Different Areas"

Objectives

The study purports to realise the following objectives.

1. To study the cognitive styles of children with and without residual sight belonging to special and integrated setting.
2. To study the achievement of children with and without residual sight in different areas (science and social science) studying in special and integrated settings.
3. To compare the cognitive style and achievement of children with and without residual sight studying in special and integrated settings.

Hypothesis

Considering the objectives of the study and the review of related literature the following hypotheses are proposed to be tested.

1. There is no significant difference in cognitive styles of residual sighted children and normal sighted children studying in special and integrated settings.
2. There is no significant difference in achievement of residual sighted children and normal sighted children studying in speical and integrated settings.
3. There is no significant relationship in achievement of residual sighted and normal sighted children belonging to different socio-economic strata.

Limitation of the Study

The following were the main limitations of this study to constraints of time and resources.

1. The study is limited to cognitive styles of children with residual sight and their achievement at primary level.
2. The sample selected for this study was limited to 200 children with residual sight and 200 children with normal sight.

3. The study was conducted within geographical areas of Delhi, Dehradun and Haryana.
4. Considering the multiplicity of languages in India, the study is confined to the Hindi-speaking children with residual sight.
5. Children with residual sight are usually scattered in a very large number of schools. The indentification of such children is a serious problem because they are spread over a large geographical area. The study is confined to the children with residual sight studying in special and integrated settings.
6. The study was strictly restricted to class II and class V children only.
7. Out of several styles and curricular areas, types of cognitive styles and two subjects—language and Mathematics were selected for administration of tests.
8. As regards the statistical treatment of data only the mean, standard deviation, 't' test, chi-square, coefficient of correlation, have been used.

FUNCTIONAL ASSESSMENT OF RESIDUAL SIGHTED CHILDREN

Name of child: ______________________________

(A) *Indoors in a familiar room*

Place: ....

Date: .... Time: ....

Light conditions:

Notes for the Teacher:

Put some interesting objects on the table in the room. Ask the child to sit on a chair against one wall. Ask the child to answer the following questions and to carry out the instructions. Do not help the child, just record your observations.

(1) How many windows are there in this room?

(2) Point to the windows.

(3) Point to the door/s.

(4) Go to the door and stand against it.

(5) Point to the windows.

(6) Point to each corner of the room and tell me what there is in each corner.

(7) How many chairs are there in the room and where are they?

(8) Point to the table.

(9) Go to the table and tell me what is on it. Do not touch anything.

(10) Go back to your chair and sit down.

(B) *Indoors is an unfamiliar room*

Place: ....

Date: .... Time: ....

Light conditions: ....

Notes for the Teacher: see above

(1) How many windows are there in this room?

(2) Point to the windows.

(3) Point to the door/s.

(4) Go to the door and stand against it.

(5) Point to the windows.

(6) Point to each corner of the room and tell me what there is in each corner.

(7) How many chairs are there in the room and where are they?

(8) Point to the table.

(9) Go to the table and tell me what is on it. Do not touch anything.

(10) Go back to your chair and sit down.

(C) *Indoors in an area with corridors and stairs*

Place: ....

Date: ....Time: ....

Light conditions: ....

Notes for the Teacher:

The teacher should visit the area before carrying out the assessment. Start in the entrance hall.

(1) We are going to start at this door in the entrance hall and come back to this door. Stand against this door marked X and describe the hallway. How big is it? How high is the ceiling? How many doors are there? How many corridors lead off the hallway?

(2) Walk beside me down this corridor and tell me what you can see. Point out windows, doors and anything you find interesting.

(3) What is that? (Point to stairs up)

(4) Go upstairs and stop at the top. (The teacher walks just behind the child). Walk along this corridor and stop when you come to a door marked Y it is the … th door on the right/left. (The teacher walks just behind the child)

(5) Stand against the door. Now go back and stop at the top of the stairs down. Do not be afraid. I will make sure you do not fall down them. (The teacher walks next to the child).

(6) Go downstairs and stop at the bottom of the stairs. (The teacher walks next to the child).

(7) (Describe the route back to the door marked X). Now go back to door marked X.

(8) Let us walk over the route together from this door marked X to the door marked Y upstairs and back. I will describe the route to you as we go along.

(9) Do you have any questions? Now I want you to go from this door marked X to the door marked Y upstairs without my help. I will follow closely behind you.

(10) Now I want you to go from this door marked Y to the door marked X downstairs without my help. I will be with you on the stairs.

Additional Notes:

(D) *Out doors in a quiet familiar area*

Place: ....

Date: .... Time: ....

Light conditions: ....

(Throughout this assessment the teacher should note the child's ability to avoid obstacles and hazards, such as poles and holes in the ground).

(1) Walk from your house to Z and tell me what you see on the way. Point out houses and describe them to me—their colour, size, position of doors, windows. (The teacher walks behind the child).

(2) *a.* (where there are kerbs) Stop when you see the kerb down in front of you.

b. (where there are no kerbe) Stop when you come to the next road in front of you.

(3) Cross the road when it is safe and continue your journey. (The teacher stays close to the child).

(4) Repeat 2 and 3 for each road crossing.

(5) (The teacher points to a parked car) what is that?

(6) What colour is it?

(7) What type of car is it? - large, small, saloon, estate.

(8) The teacher points to a moving van/lorry. What is that?

(9) What colour is it?

(10) What type of van/lorry is it? big, small. (In the case of moving vehicles, more than one vehicle may have to be used for this part of the assessment)

(11) (The teacher sees a pole/post). There is a pole/post on your route, stop as soon as you can see it.

(The above exercises can be repeated, if necessary)

(12) Now return to your house.

Additional Notes:

(E) *Outdoors in a quiet, unfamiliar area*

Place: ....

Date: .... Time: ....

Light conditions: ....

Teach the child a route from a particular house to a nearby shop and back using two or three road crossings in four stages:

(1) Introduction to route—teacher and child walking together.

(2) Revision of route—teacher and child walking together.

(3) Verbal revision of route.

(4) The child is asked to do the route without help—the teacher follows closely and makes notes on:

  a. the child's ability to travel safely;

  b. the child's ability to follow the route.

(F) *Outdoors in a busy shopping area*

Place: ....

Date: .... Time: ....

Light conditions: ....

(Throughout this assessment the teacher should note the child's ability to cope with crowds of people, as well as avoid obstacles and hazards)

(1) Identify each shop by name and type in this row of 10-15 shops.

(2) Go from shop A to shop B in this row of shops.

(3) Go from shop B to shop C (outside the row of shops in (1) above. Point in the direction of C and give some idea of distance, e.g. about 15 shops away, about 50 metres away).

(4) Go from shop C to shop D by crossing road E (Point in the direction of shop D and give some idea of the distance. The teacher should stay close to the child on the road crossing).

(5) Go from shop D back to shop A (The teacher should stay close to the child on the road crossing).

Additional Notes:

Results of the functional assessment

Analysis of the above functional assessment reports should give the teacher a good picture of the child's present level of mobility. It should help the teacher to plan the child's mobility programme. By comparing the child's clinical assessment with the functional assessment, the teacher can see whether the child is making good use of his sight for mobility or whether the child needs special training to help him to use his sight more effectively.

Guidance for teachers

(1) Before carrying out the above functional assessment the teacher should consider the following points, many of which also apply to other assessments and to teaching blind children in general. The aim of the functional assessment is to find out the child's ability to use his sight for orientation and mobility—the more general assessment of the blind child is examined below (5.3.2).

(2) The functional assessment outlined in A - F above is fairly comprehensive and will need to be broken down into a number of sessions. The tasks which the teacher asks the child to carry out increase in difficulty throughout the assessment. The full assessment is therefore not meant to be carried out, except where it is appropriate for a particular child. Young children may be only ready to do parts A and B. Much depends on the age, ability, experience, confidence of the individual child. The teacher must take care in choosing the appropriate level of functional assessment for each child and must stop as soon as the child becomes nervous or lacking in confidence.

(3) The answers to the questions put in the self-assessment report may or may not be useful. Some children may quite long and detailed answers, while others may just reply with a "yes" or "not", yet others may not understand the questions. The aim of these questions is to put the child at ease in preparation for the next assessment involving practical tasks, as well as to get the child's view of his own capabilities.

(4) The functional assessment should be carried out with as few distractions as possible in the early stages, although there will of course be distractions in the later stages. There should be plenty of time available. It will not be possible to carry out the assessment all at once: a number of sessions will be needed. A young child may only be able to complete parts A and B and then do the other parts later.

(5) Always be aware of the child's level of concentration. If the child becomes tired or restless, then stop and rest or do something else. Extra time spent on helping the child to feel at ease in the first session will ensure the smooth running of later sessions, when the tasks will be more difficult.

(6) It is good for a blind child to develop listening and comprehension skills sitting at a desk but he also needs regular periods of practical activity. Be aware of the level of language you are using and make sure the child is able to understand well. When asked by their teacher to carry out a task, sighted children receive a number of non-verbal clues—a gesture ranging from an arm, hand or finger movement to a smile or the raising of an eyebrow, teachers frequently accompany a description of a task with a demonstration of it. The blind child does not receive these clues and relies totally on spoken words. Even blind children with some useful sight may not receive the non-verbal clues. Blind children may fail to understand questions relating to activities outside their experience. The teacher should make a note of those questions not understood or misunderstood by the blind child—they may be helpful in finding out gaps in the child's knowledge and in establishing the child's overall level of development.

(7) It is also important to use the language which the child understands and feels most at home with. While Hindi is the national language of India, the child may be much more fluent in another language and have a better understanding of questions and instructions in that language. Again the inability to receive non-verbal clues may make it even more difficult for a blind child to understand Hindi if it is not his first language.

(8) For the functional assessment to be useful, it requires good observation skills and accurate recording on the part of the teacher. Take care to observe the child closely when moving and record interesting findings. Make sure the child does not hurt himself.

(9) When working indoors ask the child to perform the tasks with the given level of natural light and the natural lights off. Then open doors, draw curtains, ensure windows are clean to allow the maximum amount of natural light and record any differences in performance by the child. Lastly, where rooms have a low level of natural light, put the electric or gas light on and observe any differences in performance by the child. Keep a record of the level of lighting: poor natural light, good natural light, poor electric or gas light, good electric or gas light. Electric

or gas light can be poor in a number of ways: the whole room may be dimly lit, some areas of the room may be brightly lit, while others are in dark shadow, a bright light may also have a dazzling effect. Good electric or gas lighting will have an even distribution of light throughout the room with additional lighting in areas where reading and other close work are undertaken.

(10) The above assessment form are not meant to stay always as they are: use them to begin with, then change them in the light of experience.

(11) Finally, always give encouragement to your pupils: stress what they are able to do, rather than what they cannot do. Help them to think about themselves in a positive way.

2

PLAN AND PROCEDURE OF THE STUDY

After reviewing relevant literature relating to the problem under investigation and after developing an overview of the total layout and methodology to be followed, an investigator has to take decisions, crucial for the accomplishment of the aims of his study such as research design suitable for the execution of the study. This is followed by the selection of the sample, identification of data pertinent to the study, tools required for collection of data, method of administration and the scoring of the tests and various kinds of statistical techniques to be used. The activities mentioned above comprise the design of any research study.

THE RESEARCH DESIGN

Design is a means to identify and adopt a technique most suited for the research in hand. It is the process of making decisions before a situation arises in which the decision has to be carried out. It is a process of deliberate anticipation directed towards bringing an unexpected situation under control.

According to Johoda, Deutish and Cook, a research design is the arrangement of conditions for collection and analysis of data in a manner that aims to combine relevance to the research to the research purpose with economy in procedure."

In the present investigation relationship between the value of one variable and that of another variable had to be studied. Further, the groups with difference in the extent of sight have been formed, within each group the subjects were relatively homogeneous with respect to some variables (independent variables), while it had some comparable value with respect to other groups for the same variables and were compared with the scores of dependent variables. First of all, seven types of cognitive styles were identified following the procedure described by Aggarwal (1983). On the basis of the frequencies of subjects on groups of cognitive styles, seven contingency tables (2x2) were prepared. The same sample was administered the achievement test in language and mathematics. cognitive style inventory and achievement test were administered to the total sample of children comprising 200 children with residual sight (100 boys and 100 girls) and 200 children with normal sight (100 boys and 100 girls).

Sample

For selection of the sample including institutions for the present study, the following criteria were kept in mind:—

1. As this study was designed for children with and without residual sight, studying in special and integrated settings, the investigator was free to select the schools randomly for administering the tests.
2. The convenience and co-operation of the school authorities, principal and class teachers enabling the investigator to visit the institution as often as required for the study.
3. Only 9 (nine) school from Delhi, 1 (one) from Dehradun and 3 (three) schools from Haryana were selected. This selection was made by the investigator as per her convenience.
4. Only class II and class V grade pupils were selected by the investigator.

The sample of the present study consisted of 200 children with residual sight and 200 sighted children drawn from the primary sections of senior secondary schools of National Capital Territory. Delhi, Dehradun and Haryana. Stratified cluster sampling technique was employed to select children for the sample. The number of children with residual sight is shown in Table 2.1.

TABLE : 2.1

SAMPLE OF THE STUDY CHILDREN WITH RESIDUAL SIGHT

S.No.	Schools	Class II	Class V	Total
1.	Andh Kanya Maha Vidyalaya under Blind Social Welfare	10	10	20
2.	Jormal Periwal Memorial School for the Blind	10	10	20
3.	Rashtriya Virja Nand Andh Kanya Sr. Secondary School	5	10	15
4.	Bharat Blind School, Shahdara	10	5	15
5.	Govt. School for the Blind Boys, Kingway Camp.	10	10	20
6.	Govt. School for the Blind Boys Timarpur	5	10	15
7.	National Association for Blind, R.K. Puram Sector IV	10	10	20
8.	Blind Relief Association	10	5	15
9.	Model School for Blind Children and Partially Sighted NIVH, Dehradun.	10	10	20
10.	S.D. Institute for the blind, Ambala	5	5	10
11.	Blind Relief Association, Andh Kanya Vidyalaya, Hissar	5	5	10
12.	Netraneen Kanya Vidyalaya, Mahinder Gard	10	10	20
	Total	**100**	**100**	**200**

Sighted children of the same educational level, socio-economic status and educational achievement and of children with residual sight were selected using random sampling technique. Table 2.2 presents the composition of final sample of the study.

The identification of such children can be done by the investigator herself through observation of appearance of the eye, complaints associated with the use of the eye and their seeing behaviour.

TABLE: 2.2

OVERALL SAMPLE OF SUBJECTS

S. No.	Children with * Residual Sight				Total	Children with ** Normal Sight				Total	Grand Total
	Class II		Class V			Class II		Class V			
	Boys	Girls	Boys	Girls		Boys	Girls	Boys	Girls		
1	5	5	5	5	20	5	5	5	5	20	40
2	5	5	5	5	20	2	2	2	3	10	30
3	3	2	5	5	15	5	5	5	5	20	35
4	5	5	5	5	20	5	5	5	5	20	40
5	2	3	5	5	15	3	2	3	2	10	25
6	5	5	3	2	15	5	5	5	5	20	35
7	5	5	5	5	20	2	3	2	3	10	30
8	5	5	3	2	15	5	5	5	5	20	35
9	5	5	5	5	20	2	3	2	3	10	30
10	3	2	2	3	10	5	5	5	5	20	30
11	2	3	3	2	10	5	5	5	5	20	30
12	5	5	5	5	20	5	5	5	5	20	40
	50	50	50	50	200	50	50	50	50	200	400

* Children with Residual sight = 200

** Children with Normal sight = 200

Total = 400

TABLE : 2.3

CHECKLIST FOR IDENTIFYING SCHOOL GOING CHILDREN WITH RESIDUAL SIGHT

Appearance of the eyes.

1. Eyes not appearing straight especially when the child is tired
2. Reddened eyes or eyelids
3. Watery eyes
4. Eyes in constant motion
5. Rubbing the eyes frequently

Complaints associated with the use of eyes:

1. Headache
2. Nausea or dizziness
3. Burning or itching in eyes
4. Blurred vision at any time
5. Words or lines running together
6. Pain in the eyes after close work

Seeing Behaviour

1. Does the child have rigid body when reading?
2. Does the child place head too close to book or desk when reading or writing?
3. Does the child frown when reading or writing?
4. Does the child blink excessively when reading or writing?
5. Does the child become frequently inattentive when reading or writing?
6. Does the child lose or skip his/her place while reading or writing?
7. Does the child move head or book instead of eyes while reading?
8. Does the child become fatigued while reading or writing?
9. Does the child use a finger as line marker to guide the eyes while reading?
10. Does the child close one eye when reading?
11. Does the child face problems in pointing to familiar objects in books?
12. Does the child have difficulty in pointing to the title of a lesson in bold print in the book?

13. Is the child unable to get information from the blackboard when the teacher does not speak while writing.
14. Does the child request the teacher to change his/her seat in order to see the blackboard clearly?
15. When name of a child is called out by the teacher can he / she locate the caller?
16. Does the child avoid window in the classroom?
17. Does the child face problems in location of his/her friends while playing?
18. Does the child hesitate in moving around in bright light.

Data Collection Tools

The tools used to ascertain children's cognitive style, achievement and socio-economic status are described here.

1. Cognitive Style

The Indian adaptation made by Dr. S.C. Aggarwal (1983) of the cognitive style inventory, originally prepared by Rita and Dunn (1978) has been used for the purpose of identifying the cognitive styles of different groups of children. The following eight types of cognitive styles are included in the inventory :-

1. Flexibility vs Non Flesibility.
2. Individualistic Vs Non-Individualistic.
3. Visual vs Aural.
4. Field Independent vs Field Dependent.
5. Short attention span vs Long attention span.
6. Motivation centred Vs Motivation non-centred.
7. Environment oriented vs Environment free.
8. Responsibility vs Irresponsibility.

Cognitive style inventory in Hindi consisting of 63 items is intended to measure seven cognitive style preferences. All the items admit yes or no response and the scores range from 0 to 9 for each cognitive style separately.

Making and scoring was done as per the instructions given in the manual. The reliability quotients of different cognitive style are presented in Table 2.4.

The test retest reliability co-efficients were calculated for each cognitive style. Table 2.3 indicates that reliability coefficient ranged between 0.841 and 0.912. Since the coefficients are quite satisfactory, the inventory seems to be consistent in measuring students' cognitive styles. Thus, the reliability of the inventory is beyond doubt.

TABLE 2.4

RELIABILITY OF COGNITIVE STYLE INVENTORY

S.No.	Variables	Serial	Number of the Items
1	Flexibility Vs Non-Flexibility	.884	1 8 15 22 29 36 43 50 57
2	Individualistic Vs Non-Individualistic	.912	2 9 16 23 30 37 44 51 58
3	Visual Vs Aural	.856	3 10 17 24 31 38 45 52 59
4	Field-Independent Vs Field-Dependent	.849	4 11 18 25 32 39 46 53 60
5	Short attention span Vs Long attention span	.869	5 12 19 26 33 40 47 54 61
6	Motivation centred Vs Motivation non-centred	.841	6 13 20 27 34 41 48 55 62
7	Environment oriented Vs Environment free	.891	7 14 21 28 35 42 49 56 63

2. Achievement

The following tests were used for the assessment of learning achievement of class II and class V children.

- **Class II Language Achievement Test**

For class II students a simple literacy and numeracy test based on competencies expected to be acquired by the end of class I was used. The test was developed by NCERT as a part of the Primary Education Curriculum Renewal. The test comprising 20 items requires reading of 10 letters and 10 words.

- **Class II Mathematics Achievement Test**

The mathematics test comprises 14 items related to recognition of small and large numbers, addition and subtraction.

- **Class V Language Achievement Test**

The language achievement test comprises two sections. The first section aims at testing word meaning and consists of 20 items. The second section consisting of 24 multiple choice items tests the reading comprehension.

- **Class V Mathematics Achievement Test**

The mathematics achievement test comprises 40 multiple choice items related to number, place value, addition, subtraction, multiplication, division, fraction, time and shape, weights and measures, geometry and shape.

3. Socio-economic Status

1. Upper socio-economic status group.
2. Upper middle socio-economic status group.
3. Middle socio-economic status group.
4. Lower middle socio-economic status group.
5. Lower socio-economic status group.

For the above classification, Dr. B. Kuppuswamy's socio-economic status scale (urban) revised and modified (1977) by Dr. B. Parashivamurthy was used. Since in the present study there was no student with S.E.S. score below 5, only four groups were taken into consideration.

The coefficient of correlation 'r' is calculated between achievement in language and mathematics and socio-economic status separately. The obtained value of 'r' is tested for significance at .05 level or .01 level of confidence.

The numerical value of 'r' is a measure of relationship between two variables. Through product moment 'r' is calculated in order to determine whether there is any relationship between the two variables.

Administration of the Tools

After getting the necessary permission from the principals of different schools in Delhi, the investigator administered the cognitive style inventory and achievement test to the students of 2nd and 5th standard. The students were given instructions on how to answer various statements of cognitive style inventory and achievement test. The students were requested to ask the investigators to clear their doubts, if any. The sequence of test administration was kept uniform for all subjects.

The cyclostyled achievement test paper itself contained the bio-data form. So the pupils/students were requested to fill the necessary Bio-data in the question paper herself. The unfilled bio-data forms were filled by the investigator itself with the help of information contained in the admission register of the students in some of the schools as most of the students did not know their father's education and monthly income. The present investigator also took it as an independent variable in her study and collected the necessary data.

Statistical Techniques Used

After completion of data collection, the investigator scored performance of the students in their test by using a well prepared scoring key. After scoring, the data were tabulated for analysis for which the following statistical techniques were used.

1. Measures of central tendency and SD were calculated to know about the nature of the scores on different variables.
2. The 't' test technique was adopted to find out whether there is any significant difference between the means of all the groups which had to be compared.
3. Chi square (x^2) was calculated to ascertain the significance of differences in respect of various groups in relation to the cognitive style.
4. The product moment correlation coefficients (r) was calculated to find out the relationship between the achievement in language and mathematics and the other variables.

3

MICRO-ANALYSIS AND INTERPRETATION OF DATA

The value of research in education depends largely on the quality and rigour of the process through which its results are derived and then analysed, interpreted and applied. In order to derive facts and meaning, the raw scores were analysed and interpreted from different angles. To test the hypotheses, the data on different variables in different combinations were subjected to detailed analysis.

It has been considered desirable to present the results of the descriptive statistics in terms of Mean and Standard Diviation regarding the various measures included in this study before presenting the detailed results related to the hypotheses.

In this chapter analysis of the data collected through administration of various tools has been presented in two sections.

1. Section one of the chapter deals with the hypothesis related to the cognitive styles of children with residual sight and children with normal sight studying in special and integrated settings.
2. Section two deals with the hypothesis related to the achievement in language and mathematics of children with residual sight and children with normal sight studying in special and integrated settings.

The main objective of the study was to identify the cognitive styles of children with and without residual sight belonging to special and integrated settings. To achieve this objectieve the following hypothesis was formulated.

Hypothesis states that there is no difference in the cognitive styles of children with residual sight and normal sight studying in special and integrated settings.

For the purpose of testing the above hypothesis 2×2 contingency tables were prepared by taking each cognitive style separately for both the groups of children and chi-square test was applied to test the hypothesis. The chi-square values for each cognitive style in both groups have been presented in Tables 3.1 to 3.7.

TABLE 3.1

FLEXIBILITY VS NON FLEXIBILITY COGNITIVE STYLE OF CHILDREN WITH RESIDUAL SIGHT AND CHILDREN WITH NORMAL SIGHT

Subjects	Flexibility	Non-Flexibility	Total
Children with residual Sight	120	80	200
children with normal sight	110	90	200
Total	**230**	**170**	**400**

x^2 = 280 df = 1 Sig at. 0.1 level

Table 3.1 shows that chi-square value of 2.80 with df-1 is significant at .01 level. Thus, the null hypothesis stands rejected which implies that the children with residual sight seem to be more flexible than the children with normal sight, as 120 out of 200 residual sighted children showed their preference for flexibility style, while the remaining 80 have shown their preference for non-flexible cognitive style.

It is obvious that residual sighted students are not satisfied with just what is taught to them in the classroom by the teacher, rather they exploit variety of channels of learning and they have more inclination toward experiment, discussion and personal development regarding acquisition of knowledge. They generally show more interest in consulting various types of books to obtain exhaustive information and solution of the problems.

TABLE : 3.2

INDIVIDUALISTIC VS NON-INDIVIDUALISTIC COGNITIVE STYLE OF CHILDREN WITH RESIDUAL SIGHT AND CHILDREN WITH NORMAL SIGHT

Subjects	Individualistic	Non-Individualistic	Total
Children with residual sight	130	70	200
Children with normal sight	105	95	200
Total	**235**	**165**	**400**

x^2 =10.43 df - 1 Sig at .01 level

Table 3.2 reveals that the chi-square value for individualistic Vs non-individualistic cognitive style of two groups i.e. children with residual sight and children with normal sight is 10.43 which is significant at .01 level of confidence. Thus, the null hypothesis in this case also stands rejected, which implies that children with residual sight differ significantly from children with normal sight on the individualistic Vs non-individualistic cognitive style. Children with residual sight seem to be more individualistic in comparison with children of normal sight as 130 out of 200 residual sighted children showed their preference for individualistic cognitive style, while the remaining 70 have shown their preference for non-individualistic cognitive style. Among the children with normal sight 105 out of 200 have developed individualistic cognitive style preference while the remaining 95 have developed non-individualistic style. This implies that children with residual sight give more emphasis on the use of senses except eye. It seems to affect their preference for individualistic cognitive style, as the source of knowledge is senses. If more than one sense is involed in the learning process, it will facilitate learner to comprehend the concept easily. In the case of children with residual sight a significant problem is visual fatigueness as they are able to see only large size, colours and shapes.

TABLE : 3.3

VISUAL VS AURAL COGNITIVE STYLE OF CHILDREN WITH RESIDUAL SIGHT AND CHILDREN WITH NORMAL SIGHT

Subjects	Visual	Aural	Total
Children with residual sight	105	95	200
Children with normal sight	102	98	200
Total	**207**	**193**	**400**

x^2 = 1.92 df - 1 Value not significant

Table 3.3 indicates that chi-square value for children with residual sight and children with normal sight on visual Vs aural cognitive style is 1.91 which is not significant at any level of confidence. This implies that both groups do not differ from each other with regard to this visual Vs aural cognitive style. They appear to have almost equal preference for the visual and aural cognitive style.

TABLE 3.4

FIELD-INDEPENDENT VS FIELD DEPENDENT COGNITIVE STYLE OF CHILDREN WITH RESIDUAL SIGHT AND CHILDREN WITH NORMAL SIGHT

Subjects	Field Independent	Field Dependent	Total
Children with residual sight	120	80	200
Children with normal sight	110	90	200
Total	**230**	**170**	**400**

x^2 = 2.89 df - 1 Sig at .01 level

The above Table shows that chi-square value of 2.89 is significant at .01 level. Thus, the null hypothesis stands rejected which implies that children with residual sight and children with normal sight differ significantly on the field-indepe·ident Vs field dependent cognitive style. Children with residual sight seem to be more field independent in comparison with children with normal sight as 120 out of 200 residual sighted children have developed field independent cognitive style. Among children with normal sight 110 out of 200 have the field independent cognitive style while the remaining 90 have the field dependent cognitive style which implies that residual sighted children are more inquisitive, open minded, and divergent in thinking. They are dynamic and that is why they demonstrate their preference for field independent cognitive style, instead of structured learning they want free and independent thinking.

TABLE : 3.5

SHORT ATTENTION SPAN VS LONG ATTENTION SPAN COGNITIVE STYLE OF CHILDREN WITH RESIDUAL SIGHT AND CHILDREN WITH NORMAL SIGHT

Subjects	Short Attention Span	Long Attention Span	Total
Children with residual sight	102	98	200
Children with normal sight	106	94	200
Total	**208**	**192**	**400**

x^2 = 1.99 df -1 Value not significant

The null hypothesis with regard to difference in short attention span Vs long attention span cognitive style of children with residual sight and children with normal sight is accepted as the chi-square value is 1.99 which is not significant at any level of confidence. It implies that learning is not affected by the status of sight of an individual. Children's short attention span and long attention span cognitive style is related to their interests, motivation and learning and not to their status of sight.

Table 3.6 indicates that chi-square value for motivation centred Vs motivation non-centred cognitive style for two groups i.e. children with residual sight and normal sight have come out to be 1.99 which is not significant at any level of confidence. Motivation is an essential factor in accelerating the process of learning. In fact, no learning can take place without motivation. The success of a teacher depends on his/her ability to motivate a child to learn whether the child is residual sighted or normal sighted. Therefore, children with residual sight as well as children with normal sight have equal amount of preference for this cognitive style.

TABLE : 3.6

MOTIVATION CENTRED VS MOTIVATION NON CENTRED COGNITIVE STYLE OF CHILDREN WITH RESIDUAL SIGHT AND CHILDREN WITH NORMAL SIGHT

Subjects	Motivation Centred	Motivation Non-Centred	Total
Children with residual sight	105	95	200
Children with normal sight	102	98	200
Total	**207**	**193**	**400**

x^2 = 1.99 df -1 Value not significant

TABLE : 3.7

ENVIRONMENT ORIENTED VS ENVIRONMENT FREE COGNITIVE STYLE OF CHILDREN WITH RESIDUAL SIGHT AND CHILDREN WITH NORMAL SIGHT

Subjects	Environment Oriented	Environmental Free	Total
Children with Residual sight	110	90	200
Children with Normal sight	98	102	200
Total	**208**	**192**	**400**

x^2 = 6.87 df - 1 Sig. at .01 level

Table 3.7 shows that chi-square value of 6.87 is significant at .01 level. Thus, the null hypothesis stands rejected which implies that children with residual sight and normal sight differ significantly on the environment oriented and environment free cognitive style, Children with residual sight seems to be more environment oriented in comparison with children with normal sight as 110 out of 200 residual sighted children showed their preference for environment oriented cognitive style while the remaining 90 have shown their preference for environment free cognitive style. Among the children with normal sight 98 out of 200 have shown preference for environment oriented cognitive style while the remaining 102 have preference for environment free cognitive style.

The result indicates that children with residual sight are quite sensitive to physical environment i.e sound, conversations, street noise and other destructors and prefer to learn in a quiet and congenial environment. There are other students who do not take note of such disturbances and can concentrate on their learning task without being disturbed. But their number is quite small in comparison to normal students who require peaceful environment for learning. There is need to ensure congenial environment for residual children to enable them to learn with case.

Hypothesis States that with regard to cognitive styles there is no difference between residual sighted boys and residual sighted girls studying in special and integrated settings.

The chi-square values for each cognitive style in both groups have been presented in Tables 3.8 to 3.14.

TABLE : 3.8

FLEXIBILITY VS NON FLEXIBILITY COGNITIVE STYLE OF RESIDUAL SIGHTED BOYS AND RESIDUAL SIGHTED GIRLS

Subjects	Flexibility	Non-Flexibility	Total
Residual sighted boys	65	95	100
Residual sighted girls	45	55	100
Total	**110**	**90**	**200**

x^2 = 2.65 df - 1 Sig. at .01 level.

Table 3.8 shows that chi-square value of 2.65 is significant at .01 level. Thus, The null hypothesis stands rejected which implies that residual boys and residual sighted girls differ significantly from each on the flexibility Vs non flexibility cognitive style. More residual sighted boys seem to be flexible in comparison with residual girls as 65 out of 100 residual boys showed preference for flexible cognitive style while the remaining 40 have shown their preference for non flexible cognitive style. Among the residual sighted girls, 45 out of 100 have shown preference for flexible cognitive style while the remaining 55 have preference for non-flexible cognitive style.

This implies that residual sighted boys having better ability to perform in different fields are not satisfied with just what is taught to them in the classroom by the teacher. They show more interest in consulting various types of books to get exhaustive information. On the other hand, residual sighted girls seem to be satisfied with traditionally accepted responses to learning situations.

TABLE : 3.9

INDIVIDUALISTIC VS NON-INDIVIDUALISTIC COGNITIVE STYLE OF RESIDUAL SIGHTED BOYS AND RESIDUAL SIGHTED GIRLS

Subjects	Individualistic	Non-Individualistic	Total
Residual sighted boys	65	35	100
Residual sighted girls	45	55	100
Total	**110**	**90**	**200**

x^2 = 2.00 df - 1 Value not significant.

Table 3.9 reveals that the chi-square value for individualistic Vs non individualistic cognitive style is 2.00, which is not significant at any level of confidence. This implies that both groups do not differ from each other with regard to the individualistic Vs non individualistic cognitive style. Both residual sighted boys and residual sighted girls have equal preference for individualistic cognitive style. They develop a sense of independent working, and ability to solve one's learning problems independently with confidence.

TABLE : 3.10

VISUAL VS AURAL COGNITIVE STYLE OF RESIDUAL SIGHTED BOYS AND RESIDUAL SIGHTED GIRLS

Subjects	Visual	Aural	Total
Residual sighted boys	65	35	100
Residual sighted girls	45	55	100
Total	**110**	**90**	**200**

x^2= 1.99 df - 1 Value not Sig.

Table 3.10 indicates that chi-square value for Visual Vs Aural cognitive style is 1.99, which is not significant at any level of confidence. This implies that both groups i.e residual sighted boys and residual sighted girls do not differ from each other with regard to the visual Vs aural cognitive style.

TABLE : 3.11

FIELD INDEPENDENT VS FIELD DEPENDENT COGNITIVE STYLE OF RESIDUAL SIGHTED BOYS AND RESIDUAL SIGHTED GIRLS

Subjects	Field Independent	Field Dependent	Total
Residual sighted boys	60	40	100
Residual sighted girls	50	50	100
Total	**110**	**90**	**200**

x^2= 4.00 df - 1 Sig. at .01 level.

Table 3.11 shows that chi-square value of 4.00 is significant at .01 level. Thus, the null hypothesis stands rejected, which implies that residual sighted boys and residual sighted girls differ significantly on the field independent Vs field dependent cognitive style. Residual sighted boys seem to be more field independent in comparison with residual sighted girls, as 60 out of 100 residual boys showed their preference for field independent style while the remaining 40 have shown their preference for field dependent cognitive style. The cognitive style of 50 residual sighted girls is field independent while it is field dependent of the remaining 50 residual sighted girls.

It may be argued on the basis of this finding that residual sighted boys do not always require structured learning situation and they are less affected by the field. They get ample opportunity to develop themselves academically. However, in the case of residual sighted girls it is just the reverse.

Table 3.12 shows that the chi-square value for above mentioned cognitive style i.e. short attention span Vs long attention span for two groups i.e. residual sighted boys and residual sighted girls comes out to be 1.89 which is not significant at any level of confidence. It implies that both groups i.e. residual sighted boys and residual sighted girls do not differ from each other with regard to short attention span Vs long attention span cognitive style. The two groups are almost equally divided with regard to length of attention span.

TABLE : 3.12

SHORT ATTENTION SPAN VS LONG ATTENTION SPAN COGNITIVE STYLE OF RESIDUAL SIGHTED BOYS AND RESIDUAL SIGHTED GIRLS

Subjects	Short Attention Span	Long Attention Span	Total
Residual sighted boys	50	50	100
Residual sighted girls	60	40	100
Total	**110**	**90**	**200**

x^2 = 1.89 df - 1 Value not significant.

Students preference for short attention/long attention cognitive style are related to students interest, motivation and learning. This both groups stand on similar footings.

TABLE 3.13

MOTIVATION CENTRED VS MOTIVATION NON-CENTRED COGNITIVE STYLE OF RESIDUAL SIGHTED BOYS AND RESIDUAL SIGHTED GIRLS

Subjects	Motivation Centred	Motivation Non-Centred	Total
Residual sighted boys	75	25	100
Residual sighted girls	65	35	100
Total	**140**	**60**	**200**

x^2 = 1.98 df - 1 Value not significant.

Table 3.13 reveals that chi-square value for residual sighted boys and residual sighted girls on motivation centred Vs motivation non centred cognitive style is 1.98 which is not significant at any level of confidence. This implies a that residual sighted boys and residual sighted girls do not differ from each other with regard to possession of motivation centred or motivation non-centered cognitive style.

Motivation is an essential factor in accelerating the process of learning. In fact learning cannot take place without motivation. The success of a teacher depends on his/her ability to motivate a child to learn. A greater number of residual sighted boys and residual sighted girls have developed motivation centred cognitive style.

TABLE : 3.14

ENVIRONMENT ORIENTED VS ENVIRONMENT FREE COGNITIVE STYLE OF RESIDUAL SIGHTED BOYS AND RESIDUAL SIGHTED GIRLS

Subjects	Environment Oriented	Environment Free	Total
Residual sighted boys	70	30	100
Residual sighted girls	65	35	100
Total	**135**	**65**	**200**

x^2 = 5.82 df - 1 Sig. at .01 level.

Table 3.14 reveals that the chi-square value on environment oriented and environment free cognitive style for residual sighted boys and residual sighted girls is 5.82, which is significant at .01 level of confidence. Residual sighted boys seem to be more environment oriented in comparison with residual sighted girls as 70 out of 100 residual sighted boys showed their preference for environment oriented cognitive style the remaining 30 out of 100 have shown their preference for environment free cognitive style. Among the residual sighted girls 65 out of 100 have environment oriented cognitive style while remaining 35 have preference for environment free cognitive style.

The result indicates that residual sighted boys are quite sensitive to physical environment i.e. sound, conversations, street noise and other distractors and prefer to learn in a quiet and congenial environment. There are other students who do not take note of such disturbances and can concentrate on their learning task without being disturbued. But their number is quite small in comparison to the students who require peaceful environment for learning. There is need to ensure congenial environment for residual children to enable them to learn with case.

The second objective of the study was to measure the achievement of children with and without residual sight in different areas studying in special and integrated settings. To achieve this objective the following hypothesis was formulated.

Hypothesis states that there is no difference in the class I Language achievement of children with residual sight and normal sight studying in special and integrated settings.

In order to test this hypothesis the investigator applied (t) test to ascertain the extent to which different groups of children have learnt Language and mathematics.

Language Achievement Class II

The sample comprised 400 children of class II 200 children with residual sight and 200 children with normal sight. All children were given language test having following types of items:

TABLE : 3.15

S.No.	Area	Sub-Areas	Items
1.	Letter reading	Simple letter	9
		Complex letter	1
	Total		**10**
2.	Word reading	Words beginning and ending with letter without 'Matra'	2
		Words beginning with letter without 'Matra' and ending with letter with 'Matra'	1
		Words beginning with letter with 'Matra' and ending with letter without 'Matra'	3
		Words beginning with letter with 'Matra' and ending with letter with 'Matra'	4
	Total		**10**
	Grant Total		**20**

The mean achievement scores of the sample class II children with residual sight and normal sight studying in special and integrated settings are given below.

TABLE : 3.16

MEAN ACHIEVEMENT SCORES OF CLASS II CHILDREN IN LANGUAGE

Subject	N	Mean	SD	't' value
Residual sighted children	200	39.93	15.62	2.58*
Children with normal sight	200	56.93	15.55	

* Significant at .01 level.

Table 3.16 indicates that the mean achievement scores in language test (test reading and word reading) of children with residual sight and children with normal sight are 39.93 and 56.93 respectively.

The calculated 't' value is significant at .01 level of significance. Therefore, the null hypothesis that there is no significant difference in language achievement of children with residual sight and children with normal sight stands rejected. Children with residual sight and children with normal sight have different levels of achievement in language. Children with normal sight get more and better quality experiences from the environment which are conducive for language learning. On the other hand, children with residual sight can achieve only a limited success in language learning because they get only limited number of experiences because of their handicap.

TABLE : 3.17

MEAN ACHIEVEMENT SCORES OF CLASS II CHILDREN IN LANGUAGE

Subject	N	Mean	SD	't' value
Residual sighted boys	100	40.65	14.76	1.96*
Residual sighted girls	100	37.46	16.2	

* Significant at .05 level.

Table 3.17 reveals that the mean achievement scores in language i.e. letter reading and word reading of residual sighted boys and residual sighted girls are 40.65 and 37.46 respectively.

The calculated 't' value is significant at .05 level. Therefore, null hypothesis that there is no significant difference in language achievement of children with residual sighted boys and residual sighted girls stands rejected. The achievement of residual sighted boys in language (letter reading and words reading) is better than that of residual sighted girls. Language learning depends on the quantity and quality of experience one gets from the environment. Obviously boys with residual sight manage to obtain more experiences from the environment. Obviously boys with residual sight manage to obtain more experiences from the environment than the residual girls can manage.

TABLE : 3.18

MEAN ACHIEVEMENT SCORES OF CLASS II CHILDREN IN LANGUAGE

Subject	N	(School wise) Mean	SD	't' value
Residual sighted boys in special schools.	50	2.90	1.62	3.02*
Residual sighted boys in integrated schools.	50	6.40	1.52	
Total	**100**			

* Significent at 0.1 level.

Table 3.18 indicates that the mean achievement scores in language (letter reading and word reading) of residual boys studying in special and integrated schools are 22.90 and 36.40 respectively. The calculated 't' value is significant at .01 level of confidence. Therefore, null hypothesis that there is no difference between residual boys studying in special and integrated settings stands rejected.

It is obvious that the achievement of residual boys studying in integrated settings is higher than that of residual boys studying in special schools. This may be due to the fact that in integrated settings residual sighted children get more opportunities to interact with normal sighted children while in the special schools their exposure is limited to a particular type of children only. Interaction with children of normal sight proves to be a rich source of experience conducive for language learning.

TABLE 3.19

MEAN ACHIEVEMENT SCORES OF CLASS II CHILDREN IN LANGUAGE

Subject	N	(School wise) Mean	SD	't' value
Residual sighted girls in special schools.	50	26.59	1.62	3.64*
Residual sighted girls in integrated schools	50	39.12	1.26	
Total	**100**			

* Significant at .01 level.

Table 3.19 indicates that mean achievement scores in language (letter reading and word reading) of residual sighted girls studying in special and integrated schools are 26.59 and 39.12 respectively.

The calculated 't' value is significant at .01 level of confidence. Therefore, null hypothesis that there is no difference between residual sighted girls studying in special and integrated settings stands rejected. It is obvious that the achievement of residual sighted girls studying in integrated settings is higher than that of residual sighted girls studying in special schools. This may be due to the fact that in integrated settings residual sighted children get more opportunties to interact with normal sighted children while in the special schools their exposure is limited to a particular type of children only.

The achievement in language learning of both residual boys and girls studying in integrated setting is higher than that of boys and girls studying in special school.

Hypothesis states that there is no difference in the class II mathematics achievement of children with residual sight and normal sight studying in special & integrated settings.

In order to test this hypothesis the investigator applied 't' test to ascertain the extent to which different groups of children have learnt Mathematics.

Mathematics Achievement Class II

To assess the achievement of class II children in Mathematics a simple numeracy test comprising 14 items related to number recognition and subtraction was administered to 400 children. Details of the type of items is given below.

TABLE : 3.20

CLASS II MATHEMATICS TEST PROFILE

S. No.	Area Sub-Areas	Items
1.	Recognition of small Pairs of one digit	1
	and large number pairs of two digit number.	4
	Pairs of two digit and one digit number.	1
2.	Addition of one digit numbers.	2
	Addition of one digit number with zero	1
	Adition of zero with one digit number.	1
3.	Subtraction involving two one digit number	3
	involving some one digit numbers.	1
	Total	**14**

The mean achievement scores of the sample class II children with Residual sight and Normal sight studying in special and integrated settings are given below.

Table 3.21 reveals that mean scores in mathematics (recognition, number, addition and subtraction) of children with residual sight and children with normal sight are 39.99 and 56.62 respectively.

TABLE : 3.21

MEAN ACHIEVEMENT SCORES OF CLASS II CHILDREN IN MATHEMATICS

Subject	N	Mean	SD	't' value
Children with residual sight	200	39.99	15.36	13.92*
Children with normal sight	200	56.62	15.72	
Total	**400**			

* Significant at .01 level.

The calculated 't' value in respect of difference in means is significant at .01 level of confidence. Therefore, the null hypothesis that with regard to mathematics achievement there is no significant difference between children with residual sight and children with normal sight stands rejected. The achievement level in mathematics of residual sighted children is lower than that of children with nomral sight. The residual sighted children could not attempt even single addition or subtraction item correctly. This may be due to the fact that children with residual sight could not concentrate on their studies due to thèir handicap. This may also be due to non-availability of suitable instructional materials and use of teaching methods which are appropriate for visually impaired children. On the other hand, children with normal sight get full opportunities to develop themselves academically. They obtain varied experiences inside the school as well as outside the school.

TABLE : 3.22

MEAN ACHIEVEMENT SCORES OF CLASS II CHILDREN IN MATHEMATICS

Subject	N	Mean	SD	't' value
Residual sighted boys	100	48.7	12.49	9.26*
Residual sighed girls	100	27.7	14.27	

T* Significant at .01 level.

Table 3.22 reveals that mean scores for residual sighted boys and sighted girls in mathematics achievement are 48.7 and 27.7 respectively. The calculated 't' vlaue in respect of difference in means is significant at .01 level of confidence. Therefore, null hypothsis that with regard to mathematic achievement, there is no significant difference between residual sighted boys and residual sighted girls is rejected.

The higher achievement in mathematics of residual sighted boys may be the result of their interest, motivation, and varied experiences that boys can manage to obtain. However, achievement in mathematics in the case of residual sighted girls is not satisfactory. This may be due to the double disadvantage of the residual sighted girls i.e. the disadvantage arising out of visual impairment and the disadvantage of being a girl child.

TABLE : 3.23

MEAN ACHIEVEMENT SCORES OF CLASS II CHILDREN IN MATHEMATICS (SCHOOL-WISE)

Subject	N	Mean	SD	't' value
Residual boys in special schools.	50	24.90	1.72	2.90*
Residual boys in integrated schools.	50	30.37	1.54	

* Value is significant.

It is observed from Table 3.23 that mean scores of mathematics for residual sighted boys studying in special and integrated schools are 24.90 and 30.37 respectively. The calculated 't' value of 2.90 in respect of difference in means is significant at .01 level of confidence. Therefore, null hypothesis that with regard to mathematics achievement, there is no significant difference between residual sighted boys studying in special and integrated settings is rejected.

This implies that the environment of integrated settings is a vital factor for the development of handicapped children in academic areas. The higher achievement in mathematics of residual sighted boys studying in integrated settings may be due to the fact that these children get more opportunities to interact with sighted persons, while in the case of residual sighted boys studying in special settings, their interaction will be limited to the children of special categories only.

TABLE : 3.24

MEAN ACHIEVEMENT SCORES OF CLASS II CHILDREN IN MATHEMATICS (SCHOOL-WISE)

Subject	N	Mean	SD	't' value
Residual sighted girls in special schools.	50	26.37	1.95	1.87*
Residual sighted girls in integrated schools.	50	27.32	1.70	

* Value not significant.

Table 3.24 indicates that mean scores in mathematics of residual girls studying in special and integrated schools are 26.37 and 27.32 respectively.

The calculated 't' value for residual sighted girls studying in special and integrated settings on mathematics achievement is 1.87 which is not significant at any level of confidence. Therefore, null hypothesis is accepted which implies that the residual sighted girls studying in special and integrated settings stand on similar footing.

This implies that the achievement level of mathematics, in the case of residual sighted girls, studying in special and integrated setting are related to their interest, understandings motivation and learning. So an understanding of the students achievement level in mathematics at this stage will be of great interest to teachers.

Hypothesis states that there is no difference in the class V language achievement of children with residual sight and normal sight studying in special and integrated settings.

In order to test this hypothesis the investigator applied 't' test to ascertain the extent to which different groups of children have learnt language.

Achievement in Language Class V

To assess the achievement of class V children in language test was administered in two parts - word meaning and Reading comprehension comprising 20 and 24 items respectively. A detailed description of the test is given below.

TABLE : 3.25

CLASS V LANGUAGE TEST PROFILE

S.No.	Area	Sub-Areas	Items
1.	Word meaning	Antonyms	13
		Synonyms	07
	Total		**20**
2.	Reading comprehension	Factual details	17
		Inferences	06
		Central idea	01
	Total		**24**
	Grand Total		**44**

The mean achievement scores of the sample of the class V children with residual sight and normal sight studying in special and integrated settings are given below.

TABLE : 3.26

MEAN ACHIEVEMENT SCORES OF CLASS V CHILDREN IN LANGUAGE

Subject	N	Mean	SD	't' value
Residual sighted children	200	40.65	14.7	8.19*
Normal sighted children	200	57.2	15.67	

* Significant at .01 level.

It is evident from Table 3.26 that mean achievement scores in language (world meaning and reading comprehension) of residual sighted children and normal sighted children are 40.65 and 57.2 respectively. The calculated 't' value in respect of difference in means scores is significant at .01 level of confidence. Therefore, null hypothesis that with regard to language achievement there is no significant difference between residual sighted children and normal sighted children stands rejected.

The achievement of language sighted children is higher than that of residual sighted children. This may be due to the fact that sighted children get more opportunities to interact with people, books, magazines, newspapers and thus they receive varied experiences. In the case of residual sighted children, the range of experiences is because of the difficulties they face in seeing and reading.

TABLE : 3.27

MEAN ACHIEVEMENT SCORES OF CLASS V CHILDREN IN LANGUAGE

Subjects	N	Mean	SD	't' value
Residual sighted boys	100	38.74	2.89	1.92*
Residual sighted girls	100	36.3	3.27	

* Value not significant.

Table 3.27 reveals that mean achievement scores in language (word meaning and reading comprehension) of residual sighted boys and residual sighted girls are 38.74 and 36.3 respectively. The calculated 't' value in respect of difference in mean scores is not significant at any level of confidence. Therefore, null hypothesis is accepted as both groups of children stand on similar footing. Residual sighted boys and residual sighted girls have almost the same level of performance in language learning. Both the groups suffer from the same handicap and sex does not play any role in children's performance in language learning.

TABLE : 3.28

MEAN ACHIEVEMENT SCORES OF CLASS V CHILDREN IN LANGUAGE (SCHOOL-WISE)

Subject	N	Mean	SD	't' value
Residual sighted boys in special schools.	50	21.46	16.2	5.66*
Residual sighted boys in integrated schools.	50	40.65	14.68	

* Significant at .01 level.

It is evident from Table 3.28 that mean achievement scores of language (word meaning and reading comprehension) for residual boys studying in special and integrated settings are 21.46 and 40.65 respectively. The calculated 't' value in respect of difference in mean scores is significant at .01 level of confidence. Therefore, null hypothesis that there is no significant difference in language achievement of residual boys studying in special and integrated schools stands rejected.

The higher achievement in language of residual sighted boys studying in integrated settings may be due to the fact that they get more opportunities to interact with sighted children, while the residual boys studying in special settings get limited exposure and opportunities to interact with a large number of people.

TABLE : 3.29

MEAN ACHIEVEMENT SCORES OF CLASS V CHILDREN IN LANGUAGE (SCHOOL-WISE)

Subject	N	Mean	SD	't' value
Residual girls in special schools.	50	26.59	1.62	1.64*
Residual girls in integrated schools.	50	27.12	1.26	

* Value not significant.

Table 3.29 reveals that mean scores in language achievement (word reading and reading comprehension) of residual sighted girls in special and integrated schools are 26.59 and 27.12 respectively.

The calculated 't' value is not significant at any level of confidence. Therefore, null hypothesis is accepted which implies that the two groups of children studying in special and integrated settings stands on similar footing.

In the case of residual sighted girls, studying in special and integrated settings is related to their interest, motivation and learning.

Hypothesis states that there is no difference in the class V mathematics achievement of children with residual sight and normal sight studying in special and Integrated settings.

In order to test this hypothesis the investigator applied 't' test to ascertain the extent to which different groups of children have learnt Mathematics.

Mathematics Achievement Class V

To assess the achievement of class V children in mathematics test comprising 40 items related to number addition subtraction, multiplication weights and measures, fraction and geometry was administered to 400 children. Details of the type of items is as follows:

TABLE : 3.30

CLASS V MATHEMATICS TEST PROFILE

S.No.	Area	Items
1.	Number	2
2.	Place value	2
3.	Addition	2
4.	Subtraction	3
5.	Addition and Subsraction	4
6.	Multiplication	1
7.	Division	6
8.	Multiplication + Addition	6
9.	Weights and Measures	6
10.	Time and Period	3
11.	Fraction	3
12.	Geometry/Shapes	2
	Total	**40**

The mean achievement scores of sample of the class V children with residual sight and normal sight studying in special and integrated settings are given below.

TABLE : 3.31

MEAN ACHIEVEMENT SCORES OF CLASS V CHILDREN IN MATHEMATICS

Subject	N	Mean	SD	't' value
Residual sighted children	200	39.02	15.10	3.96*
Normal sighted children	200	59.4	16.70	

* Value is significant.

It is evident from Table 3.31 that the mean achievement scores in mathematics of residual sighted children and normal sighted children are 39.02 and 59.4 respectively. The 't' value of 3.96 in respect of difference in mean scores is significant at .01 level of confidence. The mean achievement score of sighted children in mathematics is significantly higher than that of residual sighted children. Therefore, null hypothesis with regard to achievement in mathematics that there is no significant difference between residual sighted and normal sighted children stands rejected.

It is obvious that the achievement level in mathematics of sighted children is higher than that of residual sighted children. Sighted children do get more opportunities for self study, experimentation, discussion and personal development. That is way they show higher achievement which is the result of self study and intensive practice.

TABLE : 3.32

MEAN ACHIEVEMENT SCORES OF CLASS V CHILDREN IN MATHEMATICS

Subject	N	Mean	SD	't' value
Residual sighted boys	100	29.7	1.41	4.10*
Residual sighted girls	100	20.7	1.25	

* Significant at .01 level.

Table 3.32 reveals that mean achievement score in mathematics of residual sighted boys and residual sighted girls are 29.7 and 20.7 respectively. The 't' value in respect of difference in mean scores is significant at .01 level of confidence. Therefore, null hypothesis that with regard to mathematics achievement, there is no difference between residual sighted boys and residual sighted girls is rejected. The residual boys have performed better than residual girls.

It is observed from Table 3.33 that mean achievement scores in mathematics of residual boys studying in special and integrated settings are 21.97 and 27.8 respectively.

TABLE : 3.33

MEAN ACHIEVEMENT SCORES OF CLASS V CHILDREN IN MATHEMATICS (SCHOOL-WISE)

Subjects	N	Mean	SD	't' value
Residual sighted boys in special schools.	50	21.97	1.31	4.92*

(Contd...)

Residual sighted boys in integrated schools.	50	27.8	1.42	

* Significant at .01 level.

The 't' value in respect of difference in mean scores is significant at .01 level of confidence. Therefore, null hypothesis that there is no difference between residual sighted boys studying in special and integrated schools stands rejected. The residual boys studying in integrated settings get more opportunities to interact and discuss with sighted pupils, while residual sighted boys studying in special schools are provided custodial care but out of school experience is very limited for them.

TABLE : 3.34

MEAN ACHIEVEMENT SCORES OF CLASS V CHILDREN IN MATHEMATICS (SCHOOL-WISE)

Subject	N	Mean	SD	't' value
Residual sighted girls in special schools.	50	26.59	1.59	1.64*
Residual sighted girls in integrated schools.	50	27.49	1.49	

* Value not significant.

Table 3.34 indicates that mean achievement scores in mathematics of residual sighted girls studying in integrated settings are 26.59 and 27.49 respectively.

The calculated 't' value in respect of difference in mean scores of residual girls studying in special and integrated settings in mathematics is 1.64 which is not significant at any level of confidence. Therefore, null hypothesis is accepted which implies that the residual sighted girls studying in special and integrated settings stand on similar footing.

This implies that the achievement level of mathematics, in the case of residual sighted girls, studying in special and integrated setting are related to their interest, understanding, motivation and learning. So an understanding of the student's achievement level in mathematics at this stage will be a great interest to techers.

RELATIONSHIP OF ACADEMIC ACHIEVEMENT AND SOCIO-ECONOMIC STATUS

One of the objectives of the present study was to find out the relationship between academic achievement i.e. language and mathematics and socio-economic status of children with residual sight and normal sight. To achieve this objective the following hypothesis was formulated.

TABLE : 3.35

COEFFICIENT OF CORRELATION (R) BETWEEN ACHIEVEMENT IN CLASS II LANGUAGE AND SOCIO-ECONOMIC STATUS

S.No.	Categories of Students	Coefficient of Correlation
1.	All children with Residual Sight and Normal Sight N = 400	0.84
2.	Residual Sighted Children (Boys and Girls) N = 200	0.56
3.	Normal Sighted Children (Boys and Girls) N = 200	0.58
4.	Residual Sighted Boys N = 100	0.44
5.	Normal Sighted Boys N = 100	0.57
6.	Residual Sighted Girls N = 100	0.19
7.	Normal Sighted Girls N = 100	0.30
8.	Residual Sighted Children in Special School N = 100	0.19
9.	Residual Sighted Children in Integrated School N = 100	0.46

Value (r) significant at
.05 level are 0.18 to 0.21.
.01 level are 0.22 to above.

Hypothesis states that there is no significant relationship in achievement of children with residual sight and normal sight belonging to different socio-economic status groups.

To test this hypothesis, Pearson's product moment Coefficients of correlation between the achievement scores and socio-economic status (SESR) scores of children of nine categories. i.e. children with residual sight and normal sight, residual sighted children including Boys and Girls, Normal Sighted children including boys and girls, residual sighted Boys, normal sighted boys, residual sighted girls, normal sighted girls residual sighted children in special schools and residual sighted children integrated schools with their socio-economic status groups were calculated.

1. Table 3.35 reveals that there is significant relationship between achievement on Class II language and socio-economic status of the children with residual sight and normal sight.

   The coefficient of correlation (0.84) is high and positive. This implies that a child's achievement in language goes along with his socio-economics status. The children with higher socio-economic status shall generally have higher achievement in language and vice versa.

2. There is significant relationship between achievement in Class II language and socio-economic status of residual sighted children including boys and girls.

   The coefficient of correlation (0.56) is high and positive. This implies that a child's achievement in language goes along with his socio-economic status. The children with high socio-economic status generally have higher achievement in language.

3. There is significant relationship between achievement in Class II language and socio-economic status of normal sighted children including boys and girls.

   The coefficient of correlation (0.58) is highly positive. This implies that a child's achievement in language goes along with his socio-economic status. The children with higher socio-economic status shall have higher achievement in language.

4. There is significant relationship between achievement in Class II language and socio-economic status of the residual sighted boys.

   The coefficient of correlation (0.44) is high and positive. This reveals that a child's achievement in language goes along with his socio-economic status. The children with higher socio-economic status shall have higher achievement in language.

5. There is significant relationship between achievement in Class II language and socio-economic status of the normal sighted boys.

   The coefficient of correlation (0.57) is high positive. This implies that a child's achievement in language goes along with his socio-economic status. The children with higher socio-economic status shall have higher achievement in language.

6. There is significant relationship between achievement in Class II language and socio-economic status of the Residual sighted girls.

   The coefficient of correlation (0.19) is low positive. This reveals that a child's achievement goes along with his socio-economic status. The children with middle socio-economic status shall have lower achievement in language.

7. There is significant relationship between achievement in Class II language and socio-economic status of the normal sighted girls.

   The coefficient of correlation (0.30) is moderately positive. This implies that a child's achievement goes along with his socio-economic status. The children with middle socio-economic status shall have middle achievement in language.

8. There is significant relationship between achievement in Class II language and socio-economic status of the residual sighted children studying in special schools.

   The coefficient of correlation (0.19) is low positive. This implies that a child's achievement goes along with his socio-economic status. The children with lower socio-economic status shall generally have lower achievement in language.

9. There is significant relationship between achievement in Class II language and socio-economic status of the residual sighted children studying in integrated schools.

The coefficient of correlation (0.46) is high positive. This implies that a child's achievement goes along with his socio-economic status. The children with higher socio-economic status shall generally have higher achievement in language.

This may be due to the fact that socio-economic status of the pupils significantly influences their achievement. Upper socio-economic status pupils one high achievers while low achiever are from low socio-economic status.

The above Table 3.35 reveals that in the case of residual sighted children and normal sighted children in the total sample there is significant positive correlation between achievement in language and socio-economic status. It is also true in the case of, residual sighted boys and normal sighted boys. However, in the case of residual boys and residual girls, coefficient of correlation, though positive and significant, is not as high as it is in the case of normal sighted boys and girls. This may be due to the fact that partial sight proves a stumbling block inspite of better socio-economic status. Likewise, coefficient of correlation between achievement and socio-economic status in the case of children achievement and socio-economic status in the case of children studying in special school is less than the coefficient of correlation in the case of children in integrated schools. This implies that residual sight reduces the effect of socio-economic status if they study in special schools.

TABLE 3.36

COEFFICIENT OF CORRELATION (R) BETWEEN ACHIEVEMENT IN CLASS II MATHEMATICS AND SOCIO-ECONOMIC STATUS.

S.No.	Categories of Students	Coefficient of Correlation
1.	All children with Residual Sight and Normal Sight N = 400	0.70
2.	Residual Sighted Children (Boys and Girls) N = 200	0.58
3.	Normal Sighted Children (Boys and Girls) N = 200*(Contd.)*	0.68
4.	Residual Sighted Boys N =100	0.51

(Contd...)

5.	Normal Sighted Boys N = 100	0.69
6.	Residual Sighted Girls N = 100	0.20
7.	Normal Sighted Girls N = 100	0.32
8.	Residual sighted Children in Special School N = 100	0.28
9.	Residual sighted Children in Integrated School N = 100	0.69

Value (r) significant at
.05 level are 0.18 to 0.21.
.01 level are 0.22 to above.

1. Table 3.36 reveals that there is significant relationship between achievement in Class II mathematics and socio-economic status of the children with residual sight and normal sight.

   The coefficient correlation (0.70) is high positive. This implies that a child's achievement in mathematics goes along with his socio-economic status. The children with higher socio-economic status shall generally have higher achievement in mathematics and vice versa.

2. There is significant relationship between achievement in class II mathematics and socio-economic status of residual sighted children including boys and girls.

   The coefficient correlation (0.58) is high positive. This reveals that a child's achievement in mathematics goes along with his socio-economic status. The children with higher socio-economic status shall have higher achievement in mathematics.

3. There is significant relationship between achievement in Class II mathematics and socio-economic status of Normal Sighted children including boys and girls.

   The coefficient correlation (067) is high positive. This implies that a child's achievement in Mathematics goes along with his socio-economic status. The children with higher socio-economic status shall have higher achievement in mathematics and vice versa.

4. There is significant relationship between achievement in class II mathematics and socio-economic status of the residual sighted boys.

The coefficient correlation (0.51) is positive. This reveals that a child's achievement in mathematics goes along with his socio-economic status. The children with higher socio-economic status shall have higher achievement in mathematics.

5. There is significant relationship between achievement in Class II Mathematics and socio-economic status of normal sighted boys.

   The coefficient of correlation (0.68) is high positive. This indicates that a child's achievement in mathematics goes along with his socio-economic status. The children with higher socio-economic status shall generally have higher achievement in mathematics and vice versa.

6. There is significant relationship between achievement in Class II mathematics and socio-economic status of residual sighted girls.

   The coefficient correlation (0.19) is low positive. This indicates the child's achievement in mathematics goes along with his socio-economic status. The childern with lower socio-economic status shall have lower achievement in Mathematics.

7. There is significant relationship between achievement in Class II mathematics and socio-economic status of normal sighted girls.

   The coefficient correlation (0.32) is moderate positive. This implies that a child's achievement in mathematics goes along with his socio-economic status. The children with middle socio-economic status shall have moderate achievement in mathematics and vice versa.

8. There is significant relationship between achievement in class II mathematics and socio-economic status of residual sighted children studying in special schools.

   The coefficient correlation (0.18) is low positive. This indicates that a child's achievement in mathematics goes along with his socio-economic status. The children with lower socio-economic status shall have lower achievement in mathematics and vice versa.

9. There is significant relationship between achievement in Class II mathematics and socio-economic status of the residual sighted children studying in integrated schools.

   The coefficient correlation (0.68) is high positive. This implies that a child's achievement in mathematics goes along with his socio-economic status. The children with higher socio-economic status shall generally have higher achievement in mathematics.

   This may be due to the fact that socio-economic status of the children significantly influences their achievement. Upper socio-economic status pupils achieve high scores while low achievers are from low socio-economic status.

Table 3.36 reveals that in the case of residual sighted children and normal sighted children in the total sample there is significant positive correlation between achievement in mathematics and socio-economic status. It is true in the case of other categories of children such as residual sighted boys and normal sighted boys, coefficient of correlation though positive and significant of as high as it is in the case of normal sighted boys and girls. This may be due to the fact that partial sight proves a handicap inspite of better socio-economic status. Like-wise, coefficient of correlation between achievement in mathematics like language and socio-economic status in the case of children studying in special schools is less than the coefficient of correlation in the case of children studying in integrated schools.

This implies that residual sight reduces the effect of socio-economic status if children study in special schools.

TABLE : 3.37

COEFFICIENT OF CORRELATION (R) BETWEEN ACHIEVEMENT IN CLASS V LANGUAGE AND SOCIO-ECONOMIC STATUS.

S.No.	Categories of Students	Coefficient of Correlation
1.	All children with residual sight and normal sight N = 400	0.78
2.	Residual sighted children (boys and girls) N = 200	0.68

(Contd...)

3.	Normal sighted children (Boys and girls) N = 200	0.89
4.	Residual sighted boys N = 100	0.54
5.	Normal sighted boys N = 100	0.69
6.	Residual sighted girls N = 100	0.27
7.	Normal sighted girls N = 100	0.22
8.	Residual sighted children in special school N = 100	0.66
9.	Residual sighted children in integrated school N = 100	0.84

Value (r) significant at
.05 level are 0.18 to 0.21.
.01 level are 0.22 to above.

1. Table 3.37 reveals that these is significant relation between achievement on Class V language and socio-economic status of the children with residual sight and normal sight.

   The coefficient of correlation (0.78) is high and positive. This implies that a child's achievement in language goes along with his socio-economic status. The children with higher socio-economic status shall generally have higher achievement in language and vice versa.

2. There is significant relationship between achievement in Class V language and socio-economic status of Residual sighted children including boys and girls.

   The coefficient of correlation (0.68) is high and positive. This indicates that a child's achievement in language goes along with his socio-economic status. The children with high socio-economic status generally have higher achievement in language.

3. There is significant relationship between achievement in Class V language and socio-economic status of normal sighted children including boys and girls.

   The coefficient of correlation (0.89) is high and positive. This implies that a child's achievement in language goes along with his socio-economic status. The children with higher socio-economic status shall have higher achievement in language and vice versa.

4. There is significant relationship between achievement in Class V language and socio-economic status of the residual sighted boys.

   The coefficient of correlation (0.54) is high and positive. This implies that a child's achievement in language goes along with his socio-economic status. The children with higher socio-economic status shall have higher achievement in language.

5. There is significant relationship between achievement in Class V language and socio-economic status of the normal sighted boys.

   The coefficient of correlation (0.69) is high and positive. This implies that a child's achievement in language goes along with his socio-economic status. The children with higher socio-economic status shall have higher achievement in language.

6. There is significant relationship between achievement in Class V language and socio-economic status of the residual sighted girls.

   The coefficient of correlation (0.27) is moderate positive. This implies that a child's achievement in language goes along with his socio-economic status. The children with moderate socio-economic status shall have middle achievement in language and vice versa.

7. There is significant relationship between achievement in Class V language and socio-economic status of the normal sighted girls.

   The coefficient of correlation (0.22) is low positive. This implies that a child's achievement in language goes along with his socio-economic status. The children with lower socio-economic status shall have lower achievement in language.

8. There is significant relationship between achievement in Class V language and socio-economic status as the residual sighted children studying in special schools.

The coefficient of correlation (0.66) is high and positive. This reveals that child's achievement in language goes along with his socio-economic status. The children with lower socio-economic status shall have lower achievement in language.

9. There is significant relationship between achievement in Class V language and socio-economic status of the residual sighted children studying in integrated settings.

   The coefficient correlation (0.84) is high and positive. This reveals that a child's achievement in language goes along with his socio-economic status. The children with higher socio-economic status shall generally have higher achievement in language and vice versa.

This may be due to the fact that the socio-economic status of the pupils significantly influences their achievement. Upper socio-economic status pupils achieve high scores while low achiever are from low socio-economic status.

Table 3.37 indicates that in the case of residual sighted children and normal sighted children there is positive significant correlation between class V children's achievement in language and their socio-economic status. It is true in the case of other categories of children such as residual sighted boys and girls as well as normal sighted boys and girls.

TABLE : 3.38

COEFFICIENT OF CORRELATION (R) BETWEEN ACHIEVEMENT IN CLASS V MATHEMATICS AND SOCIO-ECONOMIC STATUS.

S.No.	Categories of Students	Coefficient of Correlation
1.	All Children with Residual Sight and Normal Sight N = 400	0.86
2.	Residual Sighted Children (Boys and Girls) N = 200	0.67
3.	Normal Sighted Children (Boys and Girls) N = 200	0.87
4.	Residual Sighted Boys N = 100	0.65

(Contd...)

5.	Normal Sighted Boys N = 100	0.73
6.	Residual Sighted Girls N = 100	0.29
7.	Normal Sighted Girls N = 100	0.54
8.	Residual sighted Children in Special School N = 100	0.70
9.	Residual sighted Children in Integrated School N = 100	0.87

Value (r) significant at
.05 level are 0.18 to 0.21
.01 level are 0.22 to above.

However, in the case of residual boys and residual girls coefficient of correlation though positive and significant is not as high as it is in the case of normal sighted boys and girls. This may be due to the fact that partial sight proves a handicap inspite of better socio-economic status. Like-wise, coefficient of correlation between achievement and socio-economic status and achievement in language in the case of class V children studying in special schools is less than the coefficient as correlation in the case of class V children studying in integrated schools. This implies that residual sight reduces the effect of socio-economic status if they study in special schools.

1. Table 3.38 reveals that there is significant relationship between achievement on Class V Mathemathics and socio-economic status of the children with residual sight and normal sight.

   The coefficient of correlation (0.86) is high and positive. This implies that a child's achievement in mathematics goes along with his socio-economic status. The children with higher socio-economic status shall generally have higher achievement in mathematics and vice versa.

2. There is significant relationship between achievement in Class V mathematics and socio-economic status of residual sighted children including boys and girls.

   The coefficient correlation (0.67) is high and positive. This indicates that a child's achievement in mathematics goes along with his socio-economic status. The children with higher socio-economic status shall generally have higher achievement in mathematics and vice versa.

3. There is significant relationship between achievement in Class V mathematics and socio-economic status of normal sighted children including boys and girls.

   The coefficient correlation (0.87) is high and positive. This indicates that a child's achievement in mathematics goes along with his socio-economic status. The children with higher socio-economic status shall have higher achievement in mathematics and vice versa.

4. There is significant relationship between achievement in Class V mathematics and socio-economic status of residual sighted boys.

   The coefficient correlation (0.65) is high and positive. This reveals that a child's achievement in language goes along with the socio-economic status. The children with higher socio-economic status shall generally have higher achievement in mathematics and vice versa.

5. There is significant relationship between achievement in Class V mathematics and socio-economic status of normal sighted boys.

   The coefficient correlation (0.73) is high and positive. This implies that a child's achievement in language goes along with his socio-economic status. The children with higher socio-economic status shall have higher achievement in mathematics.

6. There is significant relationship between achievement in Class V mathematics and socio-economic status of residual sighted girls.

   The coefficient correlation (0.27) is moderate and positive. This implies that a child's achievement in mathematics goes along with his socio-economic status. The children with middle socio-economic status shall have middle achievement in mathematics.

7. There is significant relationship between achievement in Class V mathematics and socio-economic status of the normal sighted girls.

The coefficient correlation (0.54) is high and positive. This reveals that a child's achievement in mathematics goes along with his socio-economic status. The children with high socio-economic status shall have higher achievement in mathematics.

8. There is significant relationship between achievement in Class V mathematics and socio-economic status of residual children studying in special schools.

   The coefficient correlation (0.70) is high and positive This implies that a child's achievement in mathematics goes along with his socio-economic status. The children with high socio-economic status shall generally have higher achievement in mathematics and vice versa.

9. There is significant relationship between achievement in Class V mathematics and socio-economic status of residual sighted children studying in integrated schools.

   The coefficient correlation (0.87) is high and positive. This reveals that a child's achievement in mathematics goes along with his socio-economic status. The children with higher socio-economic status shall generally have higher achievement in mathematics and vice versa.

This may be due to the fact that socio-economics status of the pupils significantly influences their achievement. Upper socio-economic status pupils are high achievers while low achievers are from low socio-economics.

Table 3.38 reveals that in the case of total sample, residual sighted children and normal sighted children there is positive significant correlation between achievement in mathematics and socio-economic status. It is true in the case of other categories of children such as residual sighted boys and sighted normal sighted boys.

However, in the case of residual sighted boys and residual girls coefficient of correlation, though positive significant, is not as high as it is in the case of normal sighted boys and girls. This may be due to the fact that partial sight proves a stumbling block inspite of better socio-economic status. Like-wise, coefficient of correlation between achievement and socio-economic status in the case of children studying in special schools is less than the coefficient of correlation in the case of children studying in integrated schools. This inplies that residual sight reduces the effect of socio-economic status if they study in special schools.

4

FINDINGS, CONCLUSIONS AND IMPLICATIONS

1. Findings

The major findings of the study are as under.

Cognitive Style of Children with Residual Sight and Normal Sight

- Children with residual sight have flexible cognitive style whereas children with normal sight have non-flexible cognitive style.
- Children with residual sight prefer individualistic cognitive style in comparison to the children with normal sight who prefer non-individualistic cognitive style.
- Children with residual sight give greater preference to field-independent cognitive style while children with normal sight prefer field-dependent cognitive style.
- Children with residual sight possess environment oriented cognitive style whereas children with normal sight have preference for environment free cognitive style.
- Children with residual sight and children with normal sight have equal preference for visual and aural cognitive style.
- Children with residual sight and children with normal sight have equal preference for short attention span and long attention span cognitive style.

- Children with residual sight and children with normal sight have equal preference for motivation centred and motivation non-centred cognitive style.

Cognitive styles of children with residual sight and normal sight studying in special and interated settings.

- Residual sighted boys prefer flexibility cognitive style in comparison to the residual sighted girls.
- Residual sighted boys prefer individualistic cognitive style as compared to the residual sighted girls, who exhibit preference for non-individualistic cognitive style.
- Residual sighted boys prefer field-independent cognitive style, while residual sighted girls prefer field-dependent cognitive style.
- Residual sighted boys prefer environment oriented cognitive style whereas residual sighted girls prefer environment free cognitive style.
- Residual sighted boys and residual sighted girls prefer visual Vs aural cognitive style equally.
- Residual sighted boys and residual sighted girls prefer short attention span Vs long attention span cognitive style equally.
- Residual sighted boys and Residual sighted girls prefer motivation centred and motivation non-centred cognitive style equally.

Achievement in language class II children with residual sight and normal sight studying in special and integrated settings.

- The mean achievement score in class II language (letter reading and word reading) of children with normal sight is significantly higher than that of children with residual sight.
- Mean achievement score in class II language of residual sighted boys is significantly higher than that of residual sighted girls.
- Mean achievement scores of class II language of residual sighted boys studying in integrated settings is higher than that of residual sighted boys studying in special schools.

- Mean achievement score in class II language of residual sighted girls studying in integrated schools is significantly higher than that of residual sighted girls studying in special schools.

Achievement in mathematics class II children with residual sight and normal sight studying in special and integrated settings.

- Mean achievement scores in mathematics of class II children with normal sight is significantly higher than that of children with residual sight.
- Mean achievement scores in mathematics of class II boys with residual sight is significantly higher than of girls with residual sight.
- Mean achievement scores in mathematics of class II boys with residual sight studying in integrated settings is significantly higher than that of boys studying in special school.
- In Mathematics there is no significant difference in the achievement of class II girls with residual sight studying in Special schools and integrated settings.

Achievement in language class V children with residual sight and normal sight studying in special and integrated settings.

- Mean achievement score in class V language (letter reading and word reading) of children with normal sight is significantly higher than that of children with Residual sight.
- Mean achievement score in class V language of residual sighted boys is significantly higher than that of residual sighted girls.
- Mean achievement scores of class V language of residual sighted boys studying in integrated settings is higher than that of Residual sighted boys studying in special schools.
- Mean achievement score in class V language of residual sighted girls studying in integrated schools is significantly higher than that of residual sighted girls studying in special schools.

Achievement in mathematics class V children with residual sight and normal sight studying in special and integrated settings.

- Mean achievement scores in mathematics of class V children with normal sight is significantly higher than that of children with residual sight.
- Mean achievement scores in mathematics of class V children with normal sight is significantly higher than that of children with residual sight.
- Mean achievement scores in mathematics of class V boys with residual sight is significantly higher than that of boys studying in integrated schools.
- In mathematics, there is no significant difference in the achievement of class V girls with residual sight studying in special and integrated settings.

Relationship between achievement of different categories of students in class II language and socio-economic status.

- There exists high positive relationship between language achievement and socio-economic status of children with residual sight and normal sight.
- There exists high positive relationship between language achievement and socio-economic status of residual sighted children including boys and girls.
- There exists high positive relationship between language achievement and socio-economic status of normal sighted children including boys and girls.
- There exists high positive relationship between language achievement and socio-economic status of residual Sighted boys.
- There exists high positive relationship between language achievement and socio-economic status of normal sighted boys.
- There exists positive relationship between language achievement and socio-economic status of residual sighted girls.
- There exists high positive relationship between language achievement and socio-economic status of normal sighted girls.

- There exists positive relationship between language achievement and socio-economic status of residual children in special school.
- There exists high positive relationship between language achievement and socio-economic status of residual sighted children in integrated schools.

Relationship between achievement of different categories of students in class II mathematics and socio-economic status.

- There exists high positive relationship between mathematics achievement and socio-economic status of children with residual sight and normal sight.
- There exists high positive relationship between mathematics achievement and socio-economic status of residual sighted children including boys and girls.
- There exists high positive relationship between mathematics achievement and socio-economic status of normal sighted children including boys and girls.
- There exists high positive relationship between mathematics achievement and socio-economic status of residual sighted boys.
- There exists high positive relationship between mathematics achievement and socio-economic status of normal sighted girls.
- There exists high positive relationship between mathematics achievement and socio-economic status of residual sight girls.
- There exists high positive relationship between mathematics achievement and socio-economic status of Normal sighted girls.
- There exists high positive relationship between mathematics achievement and socio-economic status of residual sighted children in special schools.
- There exists high positive relationship between mathematics achievement and socio-economic status of residual Sighted children in integrated schools.

Relationship between achievement of different categories of students in class V language and scoio-economic status.

- There exists high positive relationship language achievement and socio-economic status of children with residual sight and normal sight.
- There exists high positive relationship language achievement and socio-economic status of children with residual sight including boys and girls.
- There exists high positive relationship language achievement and socio-economic status of normal sighted children including boys and girls.
- There exists high positive relationship language achievement and socio-economic status of residual sighted boys.
- There exists high positive relationship language achievement and socio-economic status of normal sighted boys.
- There exists high positive relationship language achievement and socio-economic status of residual sighted girls.
- There exists high positive relationship language achievement and socio-economic status of normal sighted girls.
- There exists high positive relationship language achievement and socio-economic status of residual sighted children in special schools.
- There exists high positive relationship language achievement and socio-economic status of residual sighted in integrated schools.

Relationship between achievement of different categories of students on class V mathematics and socio-economic status.

- There exists high positive relationship between mathematics achievement and socio-economic status of children with residual sight and normal sight.
- There exists high positive relationship between mathematics achievement and socio-economic status of residual sighted children including boys and girls.

- There exists high positive relationship between mathematics achievement and socio-economic status of normal sighted children including boys and girls.
- There exists high positive relationship between mathematics achievement and socio-economic status of residual sighted boys.
- There exists high positive relationship between mathematics achievement and socio-economic status of normal sighted boys.
- There exists high positive relationship between mathematics achievement and socio-economic status of residual sighted girls.
- There exists high positive relationship between mathematics achievement and socio-economic status of normal sighted girls.
- There exists high positive relationship between mathematics achievement and socio-economic status of residual sighted children in special schools.
- There exists high positive relationship between mathematics achievement and socio-economic status of residual sighted children in integrated schools.

CONCLUSIONS

From the above finding the following conclusions can be drawn.

1. Residual sighted children have preferences for flexible, individualistic, field independent and environment oriented cognitive style, while normal sighted children have preference for non-flexible, non-individualistic, field dependent and environment free cognitive style. The two groups do not differ from each other in the case of visual vs aural, short attention span vs long attention span and motivation centred vs non-motivation centred cognitive style.
2. Residual sighted boys have preference for flexible, individualistic, field independent and environment oriented cognitive style as compared to the residual sighted girls who exhibit preference for non-flexible, non-individualistic, field dependent and environment free

cognitive style. The two groups i.e. residual sighted boys and Residual sighted girls do not differ on visual vs aural, short attention span vs long attention span and motivation centred and non-motivation centred cognitive style.

3. Like normal sighted children, socio-economic status of the residual sighted pupils significantly influences their achievement in language and mathematics. Upper socio-economic status pupils achieve high scores in mathematics and language while low achievers are from low socio-economic status groups. However, coefficient of correlation between socio-economics status and achievement in both language and mathematics is higher in the case of children studying in integrated schools than the children studying in special schools.
4. Residual sighted children studying in integrated schools do better than children studying in special schools in language and mathematics.

Implications

The analysis of data has brought out several important findings which have a variety of implications for planning and designing intervention strategies for educating children with residual sight.

1. The result of the study indicates that most of the residual sighted students possess a flexible, field independent, independent, individualistic and environment oriented cognitive styles whereas normal sighted children have preference for non flexible, non individualistic, field dependent and environment free cognitive styles.

   Teachers teaching different subjects in lower classes will have to make deliberate efforts to design their teaching in line with the cognitive styles of residual sighted children.
2. In language children could read letters better than words. However, in this regard the performance of girls was lower than the performance of boys and twenty to forty per cent pupils could not read even a single word correctly. Residual sighted children had difficulties with more complex letters and words beginning and ending with 'matra'. A similar trend was reflected in the poor

performance seen in class V achievement scores in both language and mathematics. Low reading comprehension is a matter that majority of the residual students reported because they felt they had not been provided any aids and appliances or large print material in classes. Most of the residual students could not read and did not understand what they read.

This indicates the ineffective use of material by teachers in the class, once again pointing out the urgent need of imparting teaching to teachers working in integrated settings in the proper use of materials so as to eliminiate learning by 'Rote'.

3. The results of the present study may help the curriculum developer to think about the possible changes in the present curriculum keeping in view the cognitive styles of children.

4. It is suprising to see that large difference exists between residual sighted children studying in special and integrated settings. The least restrictive environment of integrated setting is a vital factor for the development of residual sighted children in academic and non-academic areas. Special schools children are missing the interaction with sighted peer groups and normal world experience, and provide twenty four hours custodial care and the out of the school experience is very limited for these children and sighted peers cannot frequently be brought to the special schools for tutoring reading service. The residual sighted children could also be allowed to go out with his/her sighted companion for a specific period of time in a day or a week. So he/she could enrich normal world experience which might help interaction.

5. Apart from this kind of activities should be helped the children with residual sighted and normal sighted children to understand each other. The teachers and school authorities should make necessary change for enriching the learning of children with special needs.

6. The study has its major implication in the field of educational researchers. The review of literature given in this report shows that both the field of cognitive style and achievement have great potentialities for further

researchers. In foreign countries a lot of work has been done in this area, but in India, little work has been done. The present study, it is hoped, will serve as a springboard for other studies in the area.

The extent to which a partially seeing child can adjust and achieve satisfactorily in a regular classroom is an individual matter and depends upon several factors. They include, among others, his visual acuity, his interests and capacities, his abilities degree to which he is able to orient himself to many class activities, the size of the class in which he is placed and the amount of attention the teacher can give him as one of several steps designed to help compensate for the handicap of poor vision.

Partially seeing children are very much like other children in that they have the same strong desire to take an active part on the family and social environment on which they find themselves. The same applies to class situations, they want recognition and status as members of their class groups. They must have opportunities to acquire outlets for those activities which enable them to like full and wholesome daily lives. We must recognise that along with the usual problems faced by all children, there in imposed upon these children, the additional handicap of poor vision. The combination may intensify and aggravate the social, emotional and educational problems they will encountering on their daily experiences, as they progress through school.

Role of the Regular Class Teacher

The role of the regular class teacher is especially important. The task of working with a partially seeing child presents a challenge to her in that her attitude toward the child, coupled with an understanding of the effect the visual defect has on the child's capacity to learn and adjust, will determine the case with which the teacher can help to create more meaningful learning experiences. The resourceful teacher must be alert to every opportunity to bring about active participation on the part of the child in those particular aspect of a learning situation which will best promote his growth and development. The teacher should understand that she can be most effective on her efforts to satisfy the needs of the partially seeing child. If she fully utilises the assistance, available through a team approach whereby the parents, the school teacher, the school psychologist, the school counsellor, the supervisor , the principal and other teachers are called upon whenever their skills and knowledge can contribute to the child's total growth and development, working together, all can help the child develop. independence, self-reliance and competency.

Role of the School Teacher

Providing a two-way liaison service between the home and the school, the work of the school teacher centres around four major needs in eye health.

1. Urging parents to secure early diagnostic and treatment of eye conditions.
2. Acquainting the home and school work proper preventive measures to avoid injury and infection of the eye.
3. Explaining how conditions under which eyes are used may be improved.
4. Pointing out to parents the need for continuing medical follow up as long as indicated.

The school teacher should provide classroom teachers with an accurate Interpretation of the eye report, explaining both the diagnosis and prognosis of the eye condition, the visual acuity for each eye both before and after correction and any special percautions to be taken when assigning activities to the child, recommendations made by the eye specialist in reference to glasses and physical restrictions should also be noted and discussed with the child's teachers.

Role of School Counsellor

In the interests of the partially sighted pupil the counsellor should work. In close co-operation with the school teacher and other school health services personnel who have the responsibility for screening and interpreting vision defects and working with parents concerning such matters. He must also recognise the implications of such defects as he assists these pupils in making realistic and satifying adjustments and plans and as he cooperates with teachers, parents, admissions officers, agency personnel and employers to the end that they have a better understanding of the total potentialities and limitations of the partially sighted pupil.

Role of the School Psychologist

Whenever the services of the school psychologist are needed for any partially sighted child, it is of particular importance that the psychologist has a good understanding of the condition of vision impairment of the child. This is true whether a situation simply involves some individual testing for appraisal of proper relationship between ability and achievement, or whether it involves a wide range of other matters, such as specific learning disabilities, possibly related to the visual handicaps, or any special problems of minor or major degree of importance which may be more directly related to the visual impainment. The psychologist's findings should take into account the effect the visual impairment may have on the total adjustment of the child. Conversely, such studies can help give insight and understanding which will further assist in the total programme of help to the child, both with regard to educational planning and counselling with the child and with the parent.

Assistance from Supervisory and Administrative personnel

Supervisory staff and principal can be of assistance by making available equipment and materials used as supplementary tools by the child with limited vision. The supervisor can be most effective by coordinating the activities and contribution of each member of the team, when recommended by the eye examiner, the principal can arrange with the superintendent of schools to provide special educational services such as the employment of readers, the employment of approved teachers to give supplementary instructional services if needed and transportation to and from school.

Contribution from Other Teachers

Pertinent comments of other teachers concerning the child's development as well as records of past achievement should be noted in the cumulative record and made available to the child teacher.

The teacher of a class for limited vision is a good source of assistance and he/she may be consulted concerning problems dealing with the use of special materials, equipment and methods of teaching.

Teacher's Guidance

In the classroom it is up to you to make sure that conditions are favourable for good vision, not only for visually handicapped/partially sighted children but for all children. A list of specific suggestions follows:-

1. Do not permit the children to face any kind of bright light when they are working.
2. During class discussion and recitation, no person who is speaking should stand with windows behind him.
3. Make the best light in the room available for the children's desks.
4. Use normal daylight illumination in the classroom whenever possible.
5. Turn on the lights when needed.
6. The windows should be kept clean at all times.
7. Do not let obstructions cut down the incoming light from the window.
8. Keep the top half of the window unshaded except when the sun strikes the window directly.
9. If the classroom sometimes serves as a projection room for movies, both dark and light window shades should be provided.
10. Shades should be attached in the middle, with one going up and one going down.
11. Try to avoid glare at all times.
12. Eliminate flickering lights.
13. Ask for light coloured, flat-finished walls, ceilings and woodwork. If you have any choice,
14. Reduce the contrast between light and dark areas.
15. Eliminate large dark areas.
16. Have additional light that can be turned on as needed in strategic spots.
17. Use tilt-top desk so that book lie in a good reading position.
18. Use printed material of a good quality.

19. Teach children to read properly.
20. Teach proper eye hygiene.

Instruction in eye hygiene should include encouraging the child in good nutritional habits. Teaching the importance of keeping face and heads clean, advising about good lighting on the home and insisting on good posture. Do not allow children to lean forward, drop their heads, and slump their shudders in an effort to see more clearly, teach them not to rub their eyes, especially with dirty hands, handkerchiefs or towels; never to run while carrying pencils and scissors, and not to throw things that could damage another's eyes. Emphasize the need for visiting a doctor if they have eye trouble.

You can include many phases of eye hygiene as part of the class curriculum in english, biology health and other subjects. Making models of the eye comparing the eye to a camera and reading about troubles of the eye are useful projects.

Classroom Suggestions for Children with Impaired Vision

Classroom plans for any child with impaired vision depend upon the information furnished by the eye specialist who has examined the child. You need this information to decide how to adjust the school routine. Checking the cumulative record may be of some help, you usually should not rely too heavily upon the instructions the child gives — or even, in some cases, upon those of his parents information from these sources may be founded on medical facts.

The specialist is best able to explain the nature of the handicap and to outline your role in serving the child. In one case, the specialist may restrict the child's physical activities, banning participation in lumping, driving or games of body contact such as football.

In another case, he may limit only the amount of reading. After you make the necessary adjustments, you should treat the child as you do every other child in the class.

Certain basic rules apply to most cases of impaired vision in the classroom:

1. *Encourage the child to visit his doctor regularly*: You may want to contact the doctor to get his/her recommendations, you should do so periodically, since

his advice may change as the child's visual ability changes.

2. *The teacher, parents and doctor must all cooperate so that any children who need glasses get them and wear them as directed:* Teach the child how to keep his lanses clean, how to keep them from getting scratched, and how to wear them properly the eyes need periodic examination to determine if adjustments are necessary in the glasses.
3. *Give children with impaired vision special seating privileges — but as unobtrusively as possible* : Place them in the spot that will be best for them, seat children who are oversensitive to light farther from the windows. Some children's eyes do not accommodate to bright light well even if they are not looking directly at it.
4. *The child's reading material may have to be prepared in large clear type or in manuscript*. This will prevent the eyes train that may occur when he copies from the board or reads average-sized printing or writing. Children who have a severe visual handicap find it particularly difficult to copy and if you can make copies for them, it will help them a great deal, if you have access to a type writer with oversize type, use it for this work. You can discuss with the physician how much of this special attention is necessary.
5. *Some children may need very black lead pencils and dull, unglazed paper:* These materials provide a great enough contact between the paper and the writing to be seen comfortably.
6. *Use the best lighted portion of the board and soft white chalk to make a good contrast:* Make your writing large and clear.
7. *Allow to teach children to write larger than usual:* Perhaps an older pupil could do some of his work on a type writer with oversize type.
8. *Secure books with large print, if necessary:* If the school does not provide them you should contact the state library, local lending libraries, the state department of education, the state university or textbook companies. Such sources can either supply the books or provide information about them.

9. *Reduce the amount of homework as much as possible :* After the child has used his / her eyes all day at school, he/she should rest them and engage in other types of activities.

10. *Limit the amount of make up work following a long absence:* Children who come back to school after a prolonged illness should not be required to use their eyes too much while trying to make up the work they have missed. Certain illnesses weaken the eyes considerably, and a long period of strain occasioned by the child's trying to make up his/her school work can do them permanent damage, you must take the responsibility of limiting the time spent in make-up work for many conscientious children will not complain but will push themselves too far.

11. *Let the ears relieve the eyes as a medium for learning:* Children with impaired vision find reading a strain. Radio discussion, tape recordings and other audio techniques prove especially valuable for them.

12. *It may help if you appoint a pupil reader:* If you do so, choose a pupil in the same classroom, one who reads well and who has no difficulty getting his own work done, for the reading will take considerable time. A pupil reader relieves you of some of your extra work with the handicapped child and also relieves the child with impaired vision of excess reading. And the work gives the pupil reader valuable experience. Many times, the two children form strong bonds of friendship.

13. *Plan short work periods so that the child does not use his eyes continuously on the same kind of activity:* The child with impaired vision probably should not do any kind of eye work for over 20 minutes at a time; then a period of eye rest should follow. He can rest his eyes by consciously changing their focus, by switching to some other type of work, such as entering into discussions, or by closing his eyes to relax them.

As a class teacher interested in good vision, then, you will want to make sure that your classrooms' physical arrangements help to prevent eye strain for all the children. In addition, you will seek to provide special help for those children whose sight is not up to standard. You should also plan to teach the children how they can protect their eyes through proper use and care.

14. *Curricular adaptations* : Children with limited vision can usually participate in most class activities. Adaptations may be necessary for some children but in general their visual handicap should not be a bar to their participation. It must be recognised, however, that most of these children will need some individual instruction, especially in such subjects as reading, writing and arithmetic. Certain school subjects such as mechanical drawing and shorthand are closed to the child with extremely poor vision. It is recommended that eye specialist and school health service be consulted when planning the students course schedule.

Since comparatively few large type books are being published, the texts being used by the class may not be available in large type. These cases, it will be necessary to have some daily lesson and related materials transcribed into large type or into manuscript writing. A typewriter with large type (18 or 24 point) is especially valuable and rapid transcription of materials can be done by a member of the school's stenograph staff, when material is reproduced on manuscript. Pencils with large soft very black lead should be used and the material got up on dull, unglazed paper without lines.

In view of the scarcity of large-type books the use of magnifiers and other types of optical aids may enable the child with seriously defective vision to use materials in ordinary type. A number of magnifiers are available which make it possible for some children to use the same materials used by their classmates and thus eliminate the need to substitute materials in large type. The use of such magnification devices, however, should have the approval of the eye physician. Therefore concern has always been expressed about maintaining the usual local distance of 14 to 16 inches while reading. Today however, greater concern is expressed for making the most of whatever remaining vision of person has one can no longer justify insistence on maintaining the usual local length for a child having seriously defective vision if with a shorter local distance he can use his remaining vision more efficiently. It is recognised that problems will arise having to do with good posture, yet compromise is necessary if the child is to be able to function as a seeing child. Certainly the possibilities of using these optical devices should not be overlooked by school health personnel in exploring means of obtaining maximum refraction benefits for children having low vision.

Arithmetic— It is advisable in a subject like arithmetic to encourage the use of mental computation to avoid unnecessary writing and copying. The pupil should be required to write down only the important steps in the problem solving sequence in order to avoid fatigue.

The use of variety of objects is especially helpful. Thus the child is able to combine the use of his / her residual vision with his/her tactile sense resulting in the acquisition of broader arithmetical concept.

Partially seeing children in the lower grades can do much of their mathematics directly on the chalkboard thus by doing away with some of the copy work and the use of small paper and pencil figures.

Reading— Reading materials for all children should be carefully selected and preference given to book with large clear type and picture, adequate spacing between lines, words and letters, suitable margins, good quality without glossy finish: and maximum contrast between background and printing. Thus fundamental reading skills and maintenance of maximum visual efficiency in partially seeing children is more readily developed.

In first and second grades books which are being used by other children may be satisfactory as many books on these lines are printed in fairly large types. In other grades it may be necessary to reproduce some of the reading materials in large type. By using libraries supply of large type books in addition to texts available from commercial publishing houses, an adequate adjustment to a reading programme can be made by these children. In order to supplement the material in large type, the use of suitable audio aids should be investigated.

Art—Free creative art in large form provides an excellent opportunity for self-expression. The use of charcoal pastels, poster paint etc. is recommended, Stress large bold strokes when using crayon, chalk and paint. Finger painting and work with clay are particularly suited to the needs of children having limited vision, no time, intricate work should be undertaken, nor should copy work and drawing with an ordinary pencil be permitted.

Music — Music provides both satisfacticent release from tension for the handicapped child. It may be necessary to enlarge musical notes to a point where he can read them. The availability of musical recordings is sufficiently broad that a child can learn a variety of songs from this source and sing them in company with the other children during the music period. The recordings also provide an excellent opportunity for music appreciation. The opportunity to study instrumental music should not be denied to these children. The approach to learn to play an instrument may require a great deal of memorising on the part of the child, but it has led to a high degree of skill by many having both the interest and capacity to play a specific instrument.

Some eye conditions may necessitate physical restrictions, therefore, the school health service and the child's eye physican should be consulted prior to the child's participation in physical education activities. It is important, however, there is no instance should restrictions be placed upon a child simply because of a vision defeat, only a face eye conditions may necessitate certain limitations in a number of physical activities.

Whenever games are played as a group activity the child with limited vision should be a assigned a part or role which he can successfully carry out. If at all possible, no situation should be allowed to arise where he is compelled to be a by stander.

The child must have an opportunity to participate in some capacity in most class activities, if he is to acquire feelings of acceptance and status among the class group.

The present work has been an humble effort in taking one of the neglected sections of the society, namely education of the children with special needs. The investigator believes that the results of the study would stimulate thinking on the part of educators, planners and policy makers to devise constructive programmes for children with residual sight in order to enhance their learning. The National Policy on Education (1986) and the Centrally Sponsored scheme of Integrated Education for the Disabled Children has emphasised that education of children with special needs are to be looked upon as a professional work rather than a charitable work. Research work in this area is a constructive endeavour rather than an intellectual excerciese and workable suggestions, needs to be these for action rather than a discussion. Teachers and school authorities should take note of this kind and make necessary change for enhancing meaningful and joyful learning in children with special needs.

BIBLIOGRAPHY

Anderson R.L. and Bancraft (1952), *'Statistical Theory in Research'*, New York, MaGraw Hill.

Ashcroft S.C. (1963), *The Blind and Partially Seeing Children*. In L.M. Dunn (Ed), *Exceptional Children in the Schools,* New York, Holt.

Anderson + Ausubel (1965). *Readings in the Psychology of Cognition,* New York, Holt, Rinehart and Winston, Inc.

Atwood, R.K. (1968), A Cognitive Preference Examination. *Journal of Research in Science Teaching,* Vol. (5). 31.

Atwood, R.K. (1971), Development of Cognitive Preference Examination 'utlizing General Science and Social Science Context'. *Journal of Research in Science Teaching,* Vol. (2) pp. 273-75.

Ausubel D.P. (1978),*Educational Psychology*: A Cognitive View, New York: Holt, Rinehart and Winston, Inc.

Baker H.J. (1938) *'Introduction to Exceptional Children'*. The Macmillan Company, New Yrok.

Broverman, D.M. (1960), *'Dimensions of Cognitive Style'*, *Journal of Personality,* Vol.(28) PP. 167-85.

Bateman, Barbara (1963), 'Mild Visual Defect and Learning Problems in Partially Seeing Children'. CEC, Res. Monograph. Washington. Council for Exceptional Children (b).

Bateman, Barbara (1964), Some Educational Characterstics of Partially Seeing Children, CEC selected convention paper. Washington: Council for Exceptional Children. pp. 74-85.

Broverman. D.M. (1964), 'Generality and Behavioural Correlates of Cognitive Styles'. *Journal of Consulting Psychology,* Vol. (28) p. 48.

Barraga. N.C., (1964) 'Increased Visual Behaviour in Low Vision Children', New York: American Foundation for the Blind.

Bateman, Barbara and Wetherell, Jahisi (1965), 'The Education of Partially Seeing Children'. In W.M., Cruickshank (Ed.), Education of Exceptional Children and Youth, New York, prentice-Hall.

Barraga, N.C. (1970), *'The Utilization of Low Vision Kit'*. Louis Ville, ky: American Printing House for the Blind.

Brown S.A. (1975), 'Cognitive Preference in Science; Their Nature and Analysis." Studies in Science Education Vol.(2) pp. 43-65.

Cohoe E. (1960), 'Teaching Reading to the Partially Seeing Child'. *Exceptional Children* Vol. 27 pp. 11-17.

Carter K.D. and Carter C.A. (1975), Itinerant Low Vision Services. New outlook for the Blind. Vol. 69 p. 255-260.

Dececco. J.P. (1970), 'The Psychology of Learning and Instruction'. New Delhi: Prentice Hall of India Private Ltd.

Eakin. W.M. Pratt. R. J. and McFarland. T.L. (1961) ,'Type Size Research for the Partially Seeing Children'. Pittsburgh: Stanwix House.

Edwards A. (1969) ,'Experimental Design in Psychological Research'. New York: Holt. Rev. Ed.

Ebel. E.L. (1969) 'Encyclopaedia of Educational Research', MacMillan Co. Fourth Ed.

Ferguson. G.A. (1959), 'Statistical Analysis in Psychology and Education'. New York; McGraw Hill Book Co. Inc.

Guilford J.P. (1954), 'Psychometric Method', New York; McGraw Hill Book Company Inc.

George F.H. (1962), 'Cognition', Methuen and Co. Ltd.

Goodrich G.L. (1977), 'Training and Practice effects in performance with low vision aids: A preliminary study'. American Journal of Optometry and Physiological Optics, Vol. 53 pp. 312-318.

Hathaway. W. (1959), 'Education and Health of the Partially Seeing Child'. New York; Columbia University Press.

Inhelder B. et al (1974), 'Learning and the Development of Cognition'. Routledge and Kegan Paul Ltd.

Jose.R.T., Cummings. J. and McAdams, L. (1975), The Model Low Vision Clinical Service: An inter disciplinary vision rehabilitation programme.

Jamir, P. (1977), 'Are Cognitive Preferences just an Expression of Cognitive Abilities?' *Journal of Experimental Education,* Vol. 46, No. 2, pp. 60-65.

Kerby. C.Edith (1952), 'A Report on Visual Handicaps of Partially Seeing Children'. *Exceptional Children.* Vol.18, pp. 137-142.

Kerlinger F.N. (1973), 'Fundamentals of Behaviroural Research', New York: Holt, Rinehant and Winston.

Kogan N. (1974), 'Cognitive Styles in Infancy and Early Childhood'. John Wiley and Sons.

Kar Chintamani (1992), 'Exceptional Children: Their Psychology and Education'. Sterling Publishers Private Limited.

Lindquist E.F. (1953) ,'Statistical Analysis'. Oxford and New Delhi, IBH Publishing Company.

Lindquist E.F. (1953), 'Design and Analysis of Experiments in Psychology and Education'. Boston: Houghton, Miffin.

Lehman E.L. (1953), 'Testing Statistical Hypothesis:' New York: Wiley.

Loomis, Helen, K. and Moskwitz S. (1958), 'Cognitive Style and Stimulus Ambiguity'. *Journal of Personality.* Vol. 26, pp. 349-64.

Livingston J.S. (1958), 'Evaluation of Enlarged test forms used with the Partially Seeing'. Sight-saving Rev. 28. pp. 37 39.

Myers E.T. (1930), 'A Survey of Sight-Saving Classes in the Public Schools of the United States', New York: Nat. Soci. Prevention of Blindness.

Myers Smith H.C. (1955), 'Psychology of Individual Behaviour', McGraw Hill Company.

Mackie, Romaine P. and Cohoe. Edith. (1956), 'Teachers of Children who are Partially Seeing'. Washington: US Deptt. of Health Education and Welfare. Bull. 4.

Mueller. M.W. (1962), 'Effects of Illustration Size on Test Performance of Visually Limited Children'. Exceptional Children, 29, pp. 124-128.

Morgan. R (1965), 'Maps for the Partially Sighted'. Newletter of the Pennsylvania Council for the Education of Visually Limited Children. Vol. 6(2) pp. 4-6.

Miller D.C. (1967), 'Handbook of Research Design and Social Measurement', New York: David Mekay + Co. Ltd.

Nolan C.Y. (1959), 'Readability of Large Types; a Study of Type Sizes and Type Styles'. Int.J. Educ. Blind. Vol. 9, pp. 41-44.

Peck. O.S. (1933), 'Reading Ability of Sight-Saving Class Pupils in Cleveland', Ohio, New York: Nat. Soc. Prevention of Blindness Publication 118. (Reprinted from sight-saving Rev.)

Pintner R. (1942), 'Intelligence Testing of Partially Sighted Children'. *Journal of Educational Psychology.* Vol. 33, pp. 265-272.

Palmer O.J. (1961), 'Statistical Methods in Research', New Delhi: Asia Publishing House.

Peabody R.L. and Birch.J.W. (1967), 'Educational Implications of Partial Vision: New Findings', International Journal for the Education of the Blind. Vol. 17, pp. 21-24.

Scott. E.P. (1975), 'The Partially Sighted Children in School'. Toronto: Canadian National Institute for the Blind.

Siegel I.E. and Cocking R.S. (1977), 'Cognitive Development from Childhood to Adolescence'. Holt, Rinehart and Winston.

Swanson H.L. (1977), 'Effect of Positive Reinforcement on Visual Academic Performance with Partially Sighted Children'. Education of the visually Handicapped. Vol. 9, pp. 72-76.

Srivastava G.P. (1978), 'Development of a Socio-Economic Scale', *Indian Journal of Social Work,*. Vol. 39(2), pp. 133-38.

Walker. W.M. and Lev.J. (1965), 'Elementary Statistical Methods'. Calcutta: Oxford + IBH Publishing Company.

William, Clive: (1976), 'A Study of Cognitive Preferences'. *The Journal of Experimental Education.* Vol. 43, pp. 61-67 (Spring).

Witkin. N.A., Moore, C.A. Good Enough. D.R, and Cox, P.W. (1977), 'Field-Dependent and Field-Independent Cognitive Styles and their Educational Implications', *Review of Educational Research.* Vol. 47. pp. 1-65 Winter.